Diagnostic Reading Analysis

Manual

Mary Crumpler and Colin McCarty

Hodder & Stoughton
A MEMBER OF THE HODDER HEADLINE GROUP

Also by Mary Crumpler and Colin McCarty:
Nonword Reading Test

Orders: please contact Bookpoint Ltd, 130 Milton Park, Abingdon, Oxon OX14 4SB. Telephone: (44) 01235 827720.
Fax: (44) 01235 400454. Lines are open from 9.00 to 6.00, Monday to Saturday, with a 24-hour message answering service.
You can also order through our website www.hodderheadline.co.uk.

British Library Cataloguing in Publication Data
A catalogue record for this title is available from the British Library

ISBN 0 340 88258 1

First published 2004
Impression number 10 9 8 7 6 5 4 3 2 1
Year 2010 2009 2008 2007 2006 2005 2004

Copyright © 2004 Hodder and Stoughton Ltd

All rights reserved. This work is copyright. No part of this publication, other than the *Diagnostic Checklist*, may be reproduced or transmitted in any form or by any means, electronic or mechanical, including photocopy, recording, or any information storage and retrieval system, without permission in writing from the publisher. *Test materials, including this Manual, are specifically excluded from the reprographic licensing scheme administered by the Copyright Licensing Agency Ltd.*

Typeset by Phoenix Photosetting, Chatham, Kent.
Printed in Great Britain for Hodder Education, a division of Hodder Headline, 338 Euston Road, London NW1 3BH,
by Hobbs the Printers Ltd, Totton, Hampshire SO40 3WX.

Contents

Key features of the DRA — 4

Purposes and uses of the DRA — 4

How to use the DRA – overview — 5

Acknowledgements — 6

1 Introduction — 7

2 Administering the *DRA* — 11
   Giving the test
   Recording scores
   Diagnostic checklist

3 Accessing and interpreting the test scores — 17
   Reading accuracy
   Reading comprehension and fluency
   What the test scores mean

4 Error analysis: reading accuracy and comprehension — 25
   Using reading accuracy information
   The reading comprehension questions and answers
   Using the reading comprehension answers
   Comparing listening with reading comprehension

5 Using the *DRA* diagnostically — 37
   Reading processes
   Reading difficulty, dyslexia and specific learning difficulties
   Analysing performance
   Analysing patterns in scores
   Analysing patterns of oral errors

6 Technical information — 53
   Standardisation of the DRA
   Reliability
   Validity

References — 61

Conversion tables — 63
   Table A: Standardised scores for Forms A and B
   Table B: Percentiles for Forms A and B

Appendix *Rules for selecting the second and third reading passages* — 70

Diagnostic Checklist *(photocopiable)* — 71

Key features of the DRA

The *Diagnostic Reading Analysis* has a number of distinctive features:

- It enables the testing of both listening and reading comprehension.
- The reading passages cover both fiction and non-fiction at each age level.
- The content and non-fiction genre at each age level closely match the framework of the *National Literacy Strategy*.
- Pupils are allowed the time they require to read three passages and answer questions about them.
- Clear presentation and full-colour illustrations encourage reluctant readers to engage with the task; light tint behind the texts removes white-paper glare.
- The test contains easy-to-interpret norms for reading accuracy, comprehension and fluency/reading rate.
- There are two alternate, or parallel, forms (A and B), with reading passages and questions on both forms carefully matched in content and difficulty.
- Scoring of reading accuracy simply involves underlining the words read incorrectly in the *Pupil Record*; for reading comprehension, simply check the pupil's response against the acceptable answers listed.
- Patterns, or profiles, of reading accuracy, comprehension and fluency/rate scores provide a first-level diagnostic assessment.
- If you wish to make a fuller diagnostic assessment, recording the errors made by the pupil will enable you to identify patterns of errors and reading strategies that are not used effectively.
- The diagnostic information can be used to inform teaching programmes and to set individual targets. Chapters 4 and 5 illustrate how the information gained from the *Diagnostic Reading Analysis* can be used in this way.
- A Diagnostic Profiler CD-ROM enables you to input raw data and obtain processed information and analyses. It also allows you to store the information from each assessment for reference on future occasions.

Purposes and uses of the DRA

The *Diagnostic Reading Analysis* can be used for a number of purposes:

- to derive a standardised assessment of a pupil's reading accuracy, comprehension and fluency/rate;
- to analyse the cueing systems (e.g. phonics) that a pupil is able to use effectively and those which are either not used or are used ineffectively;

- to inform individual target setting for pupils experiencing difficulties with literacy;
- to assess progress by re-testing with the alternate form of the test following an intervention programme;
- to contribute to a detailed assessment of pupils with suspected learning difficulties, at both the primary and secondary level;
- to assess whether pupils may need special arrangements, such as additional time, in national tests and/or public examinations.

How to use the DRA – overview

First start a *Pupil Record* with the pupil's name and age.

Explain to the pupil that:

- you will first read aloud a passage and ask some questions about it for the pupil to answer;
- then he or she will read aloud three, perhaps more, different passages and answer questions on each;
- you will time how long it takes for the pupil to read each passage;
- later you will tell the pupil how well he or she has done.

Unless you know the pupil and can gauge where best to begin, you start by reading the *Listening Comprehension* passage for his or her year group or for the year group one below.

Then follow the instructions in the *Pupil Record* to go on to the appropriate *Reading* (fiction) passage.

While the pupil is reading each passage, note his or her errors in the *Pupil Record*.

As soon as the pupil has finished reading each passage, ask the Reading Comprehension questions given (with answers) in the *Pupil Record*.

You then just follow the instructions in the *Pupil Record* to see which passage to go to next (this is shown diagrammatically on page 9).

Transfer the information to the front of the *Pupil Record*, then use the conversion tables or CD-ROM to obtain the standardised scores.

Highlight the appropriate descriptions for the three results in the right-hand boxes.

Detailed guidance regarding error analysis and using the test results to inform what to do next is offered in Chapters 4 and 5 of the manual.

Acknowledgements

Our thanks go to Margaret Lorman-Hall and Tony Kiek for processing and analysing the standardisation data, to Gill Backhouse for reviewing the material and offering much encouragement and valuable advice, and to Mike de la Mare for his detailed advice on how to make use of the diagnostic information provided by the test. We are also indebted to Charles Knight of Hodder Education for his considerable help and support throughout the development of the *DRA*.

The cooperation of staff and pupils in participating schools in the trialling and standardisation of the test in Britain was greatly appreciated. Thanks go to the following:

Boughton Leigh Junior School, Warwick
Cheddon Fitzpaine Primary School, Rowford
Chesham High School, Chesham
Cheapside Primary School, Ascot
Coten End Primary School, Warwick
Clewer Green Primary School, Windsor
Dorset SENSS and participating schools in Dorset
Dr Challoner's Grammar School, Amersham
Drake Infants School, Thetford
East Brent CE First School, Highbridge
Elgar Technology College, Worcester
Friars Junior School, Shoeburyness
Goodyear's Primary School, Warwickshire
Helen Arkell Dyslexia Centre, Frensham
Hendon School, Hendon
Hilltop First School, Windsor
Icknield High School, Luton
Inclusion Support, West Bromwich
Kingsway SENSS and participating schools in Warwickshire
Kip McGrath Support Centre, Aldridge
Lisgagelvin Primary School, Londonderry
Newmarket Upper School, Newmarket
Norton Community Primary School, Malton
Porters Grange Primary School, Southend

Putney High Junior School, London
RBWM, Maidenhead
REDC, Redcar
Redcastle Furze Primary School, Thetford
Scaltback Middle School, Newmarket
SPLD service, Newport, and participating schools in Gwent
St James and St Michael's School, Barrington
St Mary & St Peter's First School, London
St Mary's Primary School, Datchet
St Paul's Primary School, Bloxham
Stanford-le-Hope Junior School, Stanford-le-Hope
Step Forward Education Trust, Chesterfield
Step Forward Education Trust, Derby
Steps, The Edgeley Centre, Edgeley
Temple Sutton Primary School, Southend
Templefield Lower School, Flitwick
The Culver Centre, South Ockenden
The Mannamead Centre, Plymouth
The Reading Centre, and participating schools in Londonderry
Ty Alpin Primary Centre, Port Talbot
Vale of Glamorgan SENSS
Wootton Warwen Primary School, Wootton Warwen
Wraysbury Primary School, Staines

1 Introduction

The *Diagnostic Reading Analysis (DRA)* is a simple-to-administer individual reading test, suitable for pupils aged from 7 to 16 years. It comprises two elements:

- a **listening comprehension** task, where the pupil listens to a short passage read by the administrator and then answers spoken questions about it;
- a **reading** assessment, giving measures of *accuracy, fluency/reading rate* and *comprehension*. The reading assessment involves the pupil in reading both fiction and non-fiction passages and then answering questions about them. The questions are asked and answered orally.

There are two alternate, or parallel, forms (A and B) of the *reading* passages, which are carefully matched in content, interest and difficulty. This allows a pupil to be assessed more than once within a school year, and enables progress to be measured. The *listening comprehension* passages are the same for both forms.

Listening comprehension

The listening comprehension element of the *DRA* serves three purposes. It provides:

- a 'settling-in' activity for the pupil, hearing an adult read aloud;
- a 'checking' function when working with unfamiliar pupils, by helping to confirm where to start the reading assessment;
- a basis for comparing a pupil's *listening* comprehension with his or her *reading* comprehension.

There are five listening comprehension passages, which have been written against age-appropriate National Literacy Strategy (NLS) criteria while also accommodating the particular needs of pupils with reading difficulties.

Reading

For the reading assessment, there are two passages – one fiction and one non-fiction – for each age/year group. This reflects the reading experiences of pupils following the introduction of the National Literacy Strategy into English primary schools in 1998 and secondary schools in 2001. The vocabulary and phonic structures used in the reading passages follow the order in which they are introduced in the NLS, but with a focus on the work for the academic year below that of the target age group. This is because the *DRA* has been designed for below- or well-below-average readers. The choice of genre of non-fiction text for each age/year group has also been informed by the NLS, so that pupils are asked to read the types of texts with which they are already familiar.

The comprehension questions for each passage include both literal and inferential comprehension. As the questions are asked and answered orally, it is possible to measure pupils' reading comprehension effectively even if their writing skills are limited. It also reduces the time for test administration and allows you to probe for a more detailed answer straightaway if necessary.

In addition to the raw scores for accuracy and comprehension, the *DRA* provides standardised scores, percentiles and age-equivalent scores (reading ages). These are based on pupils in schools throughout England, Wales and Northern Ireland. Further details are given in Chapter 6.

You can make a direct comparison between pupils' *listening* and *reading* comprehension by simply noting any differences between their scores on the listening comprehension passage and the first fiction passage they read. The two passages have been written in similar genres and are pitched at the same level of demand, and so this comparison may indicate that a pupil *either* has a general problem with understanding language *or* that the difficulty is specific to reading.

Diagnostic analysis

Diagnostic analysis can be undertaken at two levels:

- by recording the errors a pupil makes and later analysing and categorising them;
- by looking for patterns and discrepancies in the pupil's scores for reading accuracy, comprehension and fluency/rate.

Such diagnostic information can then help inform the choice of appropriate remediation strategies.

Purposes and uses of the test

The *Diagnostic Reading Analysis* provides a standardised assessment of a pupil's reading accuracy, comprehension and fluency/rate and the opportunity to analyse the cueing systems (e.g. phonics) that she or he is able to use effectively and those which are either not used or are used ineffectively. Following an intervention programme, progress can be assessed by re-testing with the alternate form of the test.

The *Diagnostic Reading Analysis* can contribute to a detailed assessment of pupils with suspected learning difficulties at both the primary and secondary level. Additionally, it can be used to assess whether pupils qualify for special arrangements, such as additional time, in national tests and/or public examinations.

Test design

All well-designed assessments allow pupils to meet some material they can do easily, some which challenges them and some that they find just beyond them. This model of test design ensures the outcome from the test gives a valid and reliable assessment without placing undue stress upon the pupil.

The *DRA* was therefore developed and standardised on the basis of pupils each being assessed on *three* reading passages, including one that they might read easily, one they might read well and one that they might struggle on. The scoring is built on the number of words correctly read. The harder passages contain more words, giving more able pupils a greater opportunity to show their true capabilities. *All* pupils should meet a passage one level of difficulty above where they are successful and thereby maximise the number of opportunities to read words. They may exceptionally meet this hardest passage first – but then should be much more successful on the second and final passages they read.

The 'decision tree' shown in Figure 1.1 illustrates how the passages provide a structured sequence to find out how well the pupil can read and understand aural and written information.

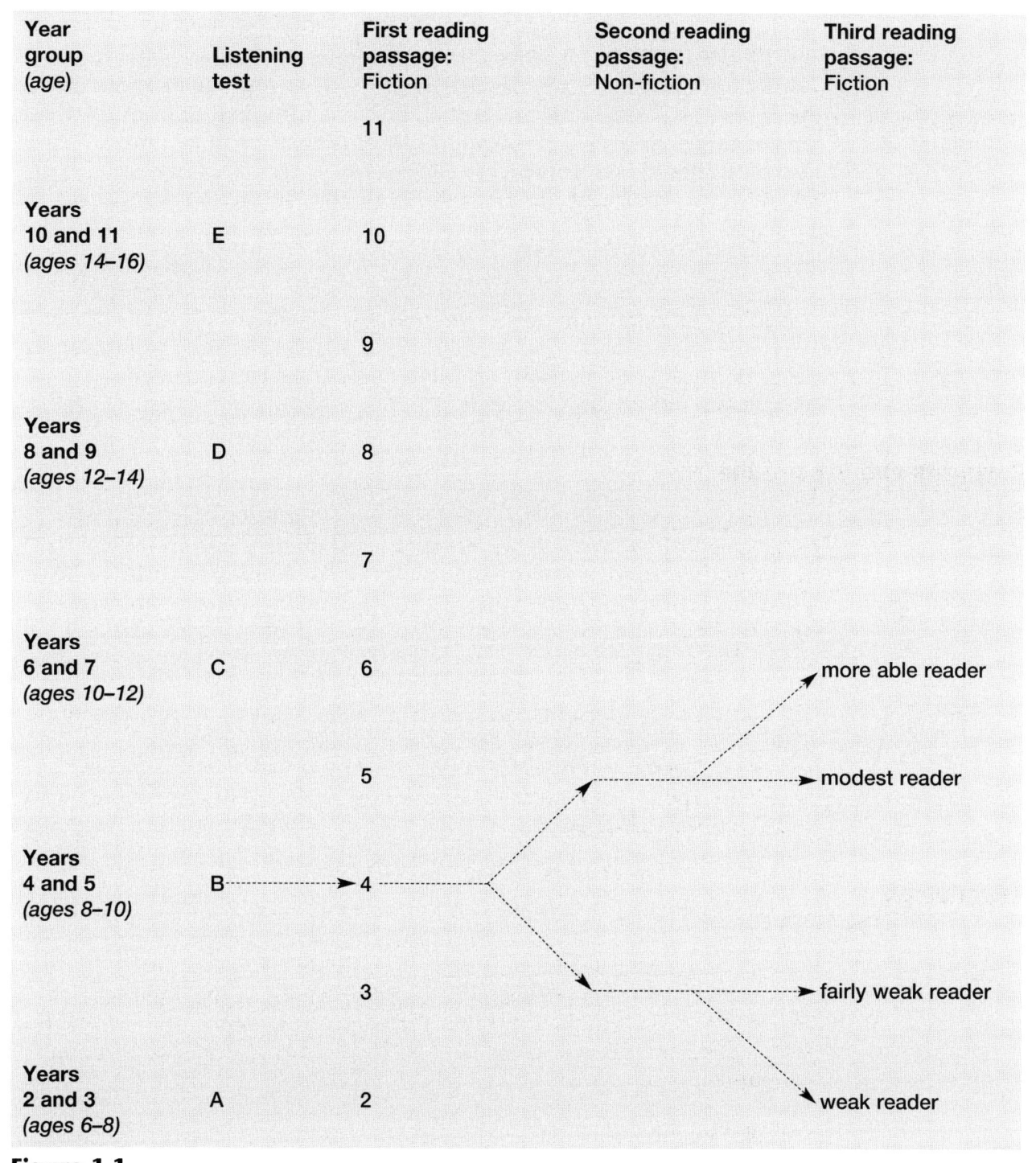

Year group (age)	Listening test	First reading passage: Fiction	Second reading passage: Non-fiction	Third reading passage: Fiction
		11		
Years 10 and 11 (ages 14–16)	E	10		
		9		
Years 8 and 9 (ages 12–14)	D	8		
		7		
Years 6 and 7 (ages 10–12)	C	6		more able reader
		5		modest reader
Years 4 and 5 (ages 8–10)	B	4		
		3		fairly weak reader
Years 2 and 3 (ages 6–8)	A	2		weak reader

Figure 1.1

Following the listening comprehension and initial reading assessment, most pupils will move up or down by one level of difficulty, and then confirm that by a further passage at the same level of difficulty. More able or very weak readers, however, will read passages at three adjacent levels of difficulty, moving up or down each time, respectively.

For example, the majority of below-average readers in Years 4 and 5 are likely to start with listening passage B. Pupils in both Year 4 and Year 5 would then normally read Fiction 4 as their first reading test passage. Figure 1.1 illustrates the progress which four different-ability readers, all starting with listening comprehension passage B, are likely to make.

When using this routine, if the pupil's chronological age and reading age are significantly discrepant, it is possible to continue with a fourth (non-fiction) or even fifth reading passage. The guiding principle is to continue testing until the pupil reaches a 10% error rate: this is always the higher error score shown for each passage in the *Pupil Record*. Where more than three reading passages are attempted, only the information from the three final reading passages (i.e. the pupil's three highest or three lowest passages) should be recorded.

2 Administering the *DRA*

Which form to use?

Forms A and B are highly reliable alternate forms, which are matched in content and difficulty, so either can be used if the pupil has not previously taken the test. If the pupil has taken the test previously, however, you should always use the alternate form. It is advisable to wait at least six months between tests if re-testing a pupil who has already been assessed on both forms.

Timing

No time *limit* is set for any part of the test. The pupil should be allowed as much time as he or she needs to attempt to read the passages and answer the questions. However, you will need to time how long it takes for the pupil to read aloud each of the three assessed reading passages if you wish to assess reading fluency/rate or use the *DRA* as a basis for allowing special arrangements in national tests or examinations.

Preparation

The pupil will need the *Reading Booklet* containing the listening comprehension and reading passages. You will need a watch with a seconds hand or display, and a *Pupil Record* for each pupil. This contains:

- the texts of both the listening comprehension and reading passages;
- the comprehension questions, with their answers;
- a space for you to record the time taken by the pupil to read each passage;
- a prompt as to which passage to go to next.

If you plan to undertake a full or partial analysis of the errors made by the pupil when reading aloud, you must be sure to note all the words that are incorrectly read. This sort of analysis is most usefully undertaken on the highest reading passage, where the pupil is likely to be experiencing difficulty and making errors. It will enable you to determine the most effective support strategies for the future.

Where to start?

The five **listening comprehension** passages (A–E) can be found at the beginning of the *Reading Booklet*. These have been written against the National Literacy Strategy for pupils in Years 2, 4, 6, 8 and 10, respectively, but also incorporate elements from earlier Years in order to accommodate the needs of pupils with reading difficulties. (Pupils in Years 2, 4, 6, 8 and 10 are aged 6–7, 8–9, 10–11, 12–13 and 14–15 years, respectively.)

- If you are testing a pupil in year group 2, 4, 6, 8 or 10 and do not know the pupil, use the passage designed for that year group.
- If you are testing a pupil from year group 3, 5, 7, 9 or 11, use the passage targeted at the year group **below**. For example, if you are testing a pupil from Year 5, use the listening comprehension passage for Year 4.
- If you know the pupil, you may wish to make a professional judgement as to which passage is most suitable and start there.

You then have a number of choices of which **reading** passage to start with:
1. You can follow the rules illustrated in Figure 1.1 (page 9), following on at the same level of difficulty from the listening comprehension passage, using the pupil's age as an indicator of where to start.

or

2. If you wish to use professional judgement because of prior knowledge of the pupil's reading ability, start with the fiction passage at one level of difficulty below where you think the pupil is, then follow the 'decision tree' criteria given in the *Pupil Record*.

or

3. If you prefer, you can start at the lowest level of difficulty and work upwards, alternating between fiction and non-fiction passages. You will then use the scores from the three highest passages.

Giving the test

Complete the pupil's personal details on the front cover of the *Pupil Record*.

Suggested wording for you to use when explaining the test is given in *italics*. You do not need to keep to this verbatim – the most important thing is that the pupil understands what to expect during the test and what to do.

Be encouraging, but do not give feedback as to whether comprehension answers are right or wrong. While pupils are reading, do not prompt or give words, but use non-committal noises, e.g. *Uhuh*.

If a partial or vague answer is given to a comprehension question, then probe to find out if the pupil can elaborate and gain credit. However, only enquire sufficiently to gain a clear understanding as to whether the pupil knows the answer or is guessing hopefully. Do not lead.

Starting the test

While we're working together, we're going to do two different things. Firstly you are going to listen to me read a short passage and then you will answer some questions about it. Then you're going to read three or more passages to me and answer some questions about them.

Check that the pupil has understood.

Listening comprehension

I'm going to read this passage to you now. Listen to it carefully and then I'll ask you about it.

Read the passage aloud to the pupil from the *Reading Booklet*. After you have read the passage, hand the pupil the *Reading Booklet* open at the appropriate listening comprehension passage. Illustrations that accompany the passages should be visible to the pupil. (Where the text and illustration appear on the same page, fold back the other passage, which appears on the facing page.)

Ask the comprehension questions and record in the *Pupil Record* whether or not the pupil has answered each one correctly. Remember to probe if a partial answer is given. Be encouraging, but do not give feedback as to whether answers are right or wrong. Do not prompt or give words, but use non-committal phrases, e.g. *Uhuh* or *Anything else?* or *So ...?*

First reading passage

Find the appropriate reading passage for the pupil to read first – this will always be a fiction text: the level to turn to is indicated at the foot of the comprehension question box on the *Pupil Record*. Then hand the *Reading Booklet* back to the pupil.

I'd like you to read this to me now. I'm not going to help you with any of the words, so try to read as well as you can. If you really can't read one of the words, don't worry, just leave it out. When you've finished, I'm going to ask you some questions about the passage. Have a quick look through the passage and start reading when you're ready. Don't worry about me timing you.

Record any errors made on the copy of the text in the *Pupil Record*. Mark as errors:

- **omissions**, where a pupil misses out a word unintentionally   **O**
- **insertions**, where a word is added   **I**
- **substitutions**, where a word is read inaccurately   **S**
- **reversals**, where two or more words are read in the wrong order   **R**
- **refusals**, where a pupil deliberately misses a word   **/**

You may also wish to make a note of hesitations, self-corrections and repetitions, particularly if you notice a significant number in any category, to provide you with extra information about the pupil's performance, but these do **not** count as errors.

If you intend to undertake an error analysis, write the pupil's exact response above the incorrectly read words, so that the information is available for interpretation later.

Time how long the pupil takes to read the passage and record this in the *Pupil Record*.

Ask the comprehension questions and record whether or not the pupil has answered each one correctly. The answers given in the *Pupil Record* are those provided by the writers of the passages, supplemented in a few instances by additional answers identified during trials. The answers given should now cover all correct responses, although you will need to use your professional judgement if a pupil gives an answer that is a synonym for one of the responses listed.

Do not alter the marking if the pupil changes answers to previous questions once you have asked further questions.

Second reading passage

Specific prompts for finding the next passage are included in the *Pupil Record*, below the comprehension questions.

The 'rules' to establish which text the pupil should read as his/her second passage are:

> **If the pupil had some difficulty (i.e. a reading error rate of 10% or more)**, the next passage should be the non-fiction text for the year/age group *below* the one the pupil has just read. (If a Year 2 pupil comes into this category, use reading passage 2: non-fiction.)
>
> **If the pupil did well (i.e. a reading error rate below 10%)**, the next passage should be the non-fiction text for the year/age group *above* the one the pupil has just read.
>
> For convenience, these 'rules' are presented as specific cut-scores on the *Pupil Record*. The complete table showing the number of errors that acts as the 'hurdle' for each passage is provided in the Appendix.

Find the appropriate non-fiction passage for the pupil to read next, and then hand the *Reading Booklet* back to the pupil.

We're going to do exactly the same with this passage. You're going to read it to me and when you've finished, I'm going to ask you some questions about it. Have a quick look through the passage and start reading when you're ready.

Mark and score errors and note the time taken to read the passage as before. Ask the comprehension questions and record the pupil's responses.

Third reading passage

The specific criteria to select the third passage are given in the *Pupil Record*, below the comprehension questions for the non-fiction passages.

The 'rules' to establish which text the pupil should read as his/her final passage are:

For the pupil who went UP one level for the non-fiction passage:

> **If the pupil had some difficulty (i.e. a reading error rate of 10% or more)**, the next passage should be the fiction text for the *same* level.
>
> **If the pupil did well (i.e. a reading error rate less than 10%)**, the next passage should be the fiction text for the next *higher* year/age group.

For the pupil who went DOWN one level for the non-fiction passage:

> **If the pupil had some difficulty (i.e. a reading error rate of 10% or more)**, the next passage should be the fiction text for the year group *below*.
>
> **If the pupil did well (i.e. a reading error rate less than 10%)**, the next passage should be the fiction text for the *same* level.

Again, these 'rules' are presented as specific cut-scores in the *Pupil Record*. The complete table showing the number of errors that acts as the 'hurdle' for each passage is provided in the Appendix.

Find the appropriate passage for the pupil to read next and then hand the *Reading Booklet* back to the pupil.

We're going to do exactly the same with this passage. You're going to read it to me and when you've finished, I'm going to ask you some questions about it. Have a quick look through the passage and start reading when you're ready.

Mark and score errors and note the time taken to read the passage, as before. Ask the comprehension questions and record the pupil's responses.

If the pupil has not yet approached the 'ceiling' of his or her reading ability (i.e. has not made at least 10% errors) on any of these three reading passages, go up to the next (non-fiction) passage, at the next level of difficulty. Continue going up, alternating between fiction and non-fiction passages, until the pupil does make at least 10% errors or until you reach the end of the test.

Recording scores

When testing has been completed, summarise the results in the relevant boxes on the front page of the *Pupil Record*. This summary can then be used to find standardised or age-equivalent scores for accuracy, comprehension and rate of reading, using the tables provided (see next chapter).

Listening comprehension

- Note on the front page of the *Pupil Record* the letter (A–E) of the passage that the pupil listened to, and the number of related comprehension questions answered correctly.

Accuracy

- Record the genre and numbers of the three passages on which the pupil is being assessed – i.e. the three most demanding passages read by the pupil (e.g. record Fiction 3, Non-fiction 4, Fiction 5 as F3, NF4, F5).
- Record also the number of words in each passage and the number of errors made. For your convenience, the number of words in the passages is noted each time, in the box where you record the number of errors after each passage has been read (e.g. for Fiction 3: Errors __ out of 40).

- Add together the number of words in the three passages read, and record this in the 'Totals' column, in the box labelled *(a)*.
- Add together the number of errors made, and record this in the 'Totals' column, in the box labelled *(b)*.
- Calculate the pupil's raw score for reading accuracy by subtracting the total number of errors as recorded in *(b)* from the total number of words read, as recorded in box *(a)*. Transfer this figure to the first row of the Reading Analysis box.

Fluency/Reading rate

- Transfer the time taken, in seconds, to read each of the three assessed passages. Add these together and record this in the 'Totals' column, in the box labelled *(c)*.
- Calculate the reading rate by dividing the total number of words as recorded in box *(a)* by the total number of seconds as recorded in box *(c)*. Multiply the result by 60 to calculate the number of words read per minute. Transfer this figure to the relevant row of the Reading Analysis box.

Comprehension

- Transfer the number of comprehension questions answered correctly for each of the three assessed passages. Add these together and record this in the 'Totals' column, in the box labelled *(d)*.

Once these raw scores have been calculated, they can be used to obtain standardised and age-equivalent scores and percentiles, as detailed in the next chapter.

Diagnostic checklist

If you wish to record and analyse *qualitative* information about the assessment, including information about the pupil's attitude and behaviour, a *photocopiable* checklist is provided at the end of this Manual.

3 Accessing and interpreting the test scores

Reading accuracy

The *Diagnostic Reading Analysis* enables you to convert the raw scores for reading accuracy into:

- standardised scores;
- percentiles;
- reading ages.

It also enables you to relate a pupil's reading age to that of others who have achieved the same National Curriculum level.

Obtaining standardised scores

Standardised scores for reading accuracy are obtained from Table A, for both Forms A and B of the *DRA*. This table may be found at the end of this Manual.

Table A provides standardised scores for six-month age categories, from 7 years 6 months up to 16 years 5 months (together with standardised scores for the full-year range 6:6 to 7:5). Age groups are given, in years and completed months, at the top and foot of each column: for example, the third age group includes ages ranging from 8 years 0 months (8:0) up to and including 8 years 5 months (8:5).

Check that the raw score and chronological age of the pupil have been correctly calculated. Locate the raw score (in the first column), then locate the column for the pupil's chronological age. Reading across the row, locate the standardised score in the column that corresponds to the pupil's raw score and record that score on the front of the *Pupil Record*. So, for example, a pupil aged 10:3 with an accuracy raw score of 145 (i.e. has read 145 words correctly in the three assessed passages) should be recorded as having a standardised score of 88.

Other measures

Percentiles corresponding to the standardised scores for both Forms A and B are given in Table B, at the end of this Manual. From this table, you can see that our pupil aged 10:3 with an accuracy score of 145 is at the 25th percentile.

Reading ages can be read directly from Table 3.1, overleaf. Here an accuracy score of 145 equates to a reading age of 9 years 0 months. (Scores cannot be provided for every month of age, as this would attribute a spurious precision to this type of measure.)

Table 3.1: Reading ages

No. of words correctly read	Reading age (years:months)	No. of words correctly read	Reading age (years:months)
<60	<5:0	180	10:8
60	5:0	185	10:11
65	5:3	190	11:0
70	5:6	195	11:2
75	5:9	200	11:4
80	6:0	205	11:6
85	6:2	210	11:9
90	6:4	215	11:11
95	6:6	220	12:3
100	6:8	225	12:6
105	6:11	230	12:9
110	7:0	235	12:11
115	7:5	240	13:3
120	7:9	245	13:6
125	8:0	245	13:9
130	8:3	250	14:0
135	8:6	255	14:6
140	8:9	260	15:0
145	9:0	265	15:3
150	9:3	270	15:9
155	9:6	275	16:3
160	9:10	280	16:4
165	10:1	285	16:5
170	10:4	290+	>16:5
175	10:6		

Reading comprehension and fluency

The raw scores for fluency/reading rate and reading comprehension can be accurately evaluated using Tables 3.2 and 3.3. For each chronological age group, these tables show the scores of pupils in five bands: *Very weak, Well below average, Average/age-appropriate, Well above average,* and *Excellent*.

These five categories correspond with those indicated for the pupils' reading accuracy (see shading in Table A). Figure 3.1, on page 20, shows how these range bands relate to the 'normal distribution' curve.

What the test scores mean

Accuracy: standardised scores

For most practical purposes, and especially for making comparisons over time, standardised scores are the best scores upon which to rely, as they are the type of score least likely to be misinterpreted. Standardised scores for the *DRA* cover the range 65–130, for pupils aged from 6:6 to 16:5 years.

Table 3.2: Fluency/reading rate and age

Chronological age	Very weak	Well below average	Average	Well above average	Excellent
6:6–7:5	0–21	22–30	31–65	66–120	>120
7:6–7:11	0–25	26–49	50–133	134–187	>187
8:0–8:5	0–28	29–41	42–153	154–187	>187
8:6–8:11	0–21	22–33	34–93	94–129	>129
9:0–9:5	0–22	23–35	36–88	89–168	>168
9:6–9:11	0–27	28–37	38–95	96–128	>128
10:0–10:5	0–30	31–49	50–117	118–136	>136
10:6–10:11	0–24	25–37	38–105	106–155	>155
11:0–11:5	0–22	23–30	31–105	106–144	>144
11:6–11:11	0–22	23–41	42–122	123–158	>158
12:0–12:5	0–24	25–37	38–122	123–170	>170
12:6–12:11	0–26	27–40	41–131	132–162	>162
13:0–13:5	0–21	22–37	38–130	131–166	>166
13:6–13:11	0–31	32–49	50–145	146–157	>157
14:0–14:5	0–26	27–44	45–135	136–164	>164
14:6–14:11	0–40	41–57	58–149	150–168	>168
15:0–15:5	0–30	31–42	43–122	123–154	>154
15:6–15:11	0–26	27–55	56–154	155–173	>173
16:0–16:5	0–39	40–48	49–148	149–180	>180

Note that the Fluency/reading rate measure is obtained by adding together the pupil's times in the three assessed reading passages, not necessarily *all* of the passages he or she has read.

Table 3.3: Reading comprehension scores and age

Chronological age	Very weak	Well below average	Average	Well above average	Excellent
6:6–7:5	0–5	6–7	8–10	11–13	>13
7:6–7:11	0–5	6–7	8–10	11–13	>13
8:0–8:5	0–5	6–7	8–11	12–13	>13
8:6–8:11	0–4	5–6	7–11	12–16	>16
9:0–9:5	0–4	5–6	7–12	13–14	>14
9:6–9:11	0–5	6–7	8–12	13–16	>16
10:0–10:5	0–5	6–9	10–15	16–17	>17
10:6–10:11	0–5	6–9	10–15	16–18	>18
11:0–11:5	0–6	7–9	10–16	17–18	>18
11:6–11:11	0–6	7–10	11–15	16–19	>19
12:0–12:5	0–4	5–10	11–17	18–20	>20
12:6–12:11	0–4	5–10	11–16	17–19	>19
13:0–13:5	0–5	6–10	11–18	19–20	>20
13:6–13:11	0–6	7–10	11–17	18–20	>20
14:0–14:5	0–4	5–10	11–17	18–19	>19
14:6–14:11	0–5	6–11	12–17	18–20	>20
15:0–15:5	0–5	6–11	12–18	19–20	>20
15:6–15:11	0–7	8–11	12–18	19–20	>20
16:0–16:5	0–8	9–13	14–19	20–21	>21

Note that the reading comprehension measure is obtained by adding together the pupil's comprehension scores in the three assessed reading passages, not necessarily *all* of the passages he or she has read.

Accessing and interpreting the test scores

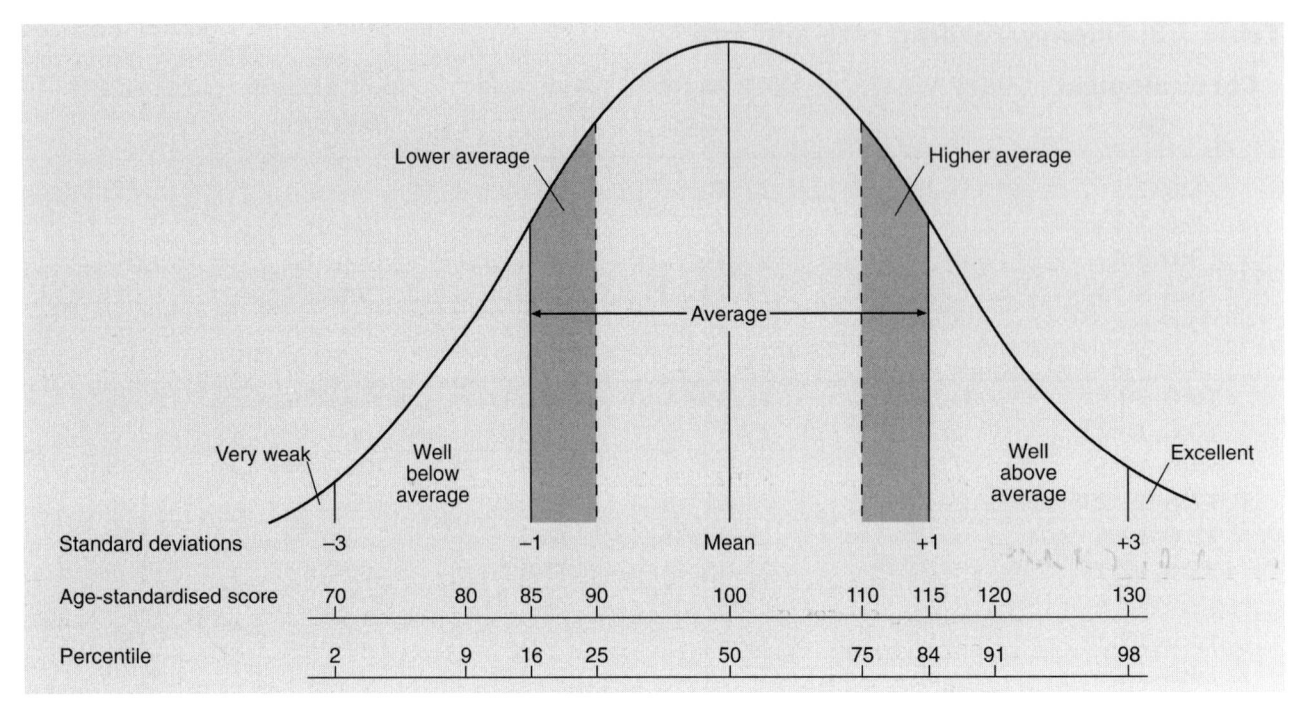

Figure 3.1

The standardised score provides important information on the extent to which pupils within each age group are performing compared with their age peers (see Table 3.4). It also provides a basis on which decisions can be made concerning the need for a particular pupil to receive extra help. The *DRA* standardisation sample was mainly drawn from weak readers, as described in Chapter 6, to provide stronger information about the bottom quartile (25%) of the normal school population. However, because equating processes have been used, the data can be reported using the usual mean of 100 and standard deviation of 15.

Table 3.4: Relationship between *DRA* standardised scores and qualitative interpretations

Standardised score	Qualitative interpretation of standardised scores	Standard deviation from mean	Percentile score	Percentage of normal population
>130	Excellent	>+2	>98	2.27
116–130	Well above average	+1 to +2	84–98	13.59
110–115	*higher average*			
85–115	Average/age-appropriate	–1 to +1	16–83	68.26
85–90	*lower average*			
70–84	Well below average	–1 to –2	2–15	13.59
<69	Very weak	<–2	<2	2.27

Because the majority of pupils fall, by definition, within the central, relatively broad 'average/age-appropriate' band, it can be helpful to identify a narrow slice at each side of the average range as 'lower average' and 'higher average': these are shown in Figure 3.1, defined by standardised scores in the range 85–90 (*lower average*) and 110–115 (*higher average*).

Lower down the ability scale, it can also be helpful in determining the appropriate next step to consider a standardised score of between 80 and 70 (approx. 1.5 standard deviations below the mean) as indicating a *moderate deficit*, and a standardised score of 69 or less (2 standard deviations below the mean) as indicative of a *severe deficit* in reading accuracy.

Standardised scores enable you to follow a pupil's progress year-on-year, as they are determined for a normal sample of pupils where the mean is 100. If a pupil's standardised score increases from one test to a subsequent one then, compared with all the pupils in that age cohort, the pupil's reading is improving.

Standardised scores may also be expressed as *percentile scores*.

Accuracy: percentiles

Percentile scores give alternative information about a pupil's performance in comparison to his or her age group. Percentiles range from 0 to 100 and indicate the pupil's position relative to the standardisation sample. Because percentiles are calculated from the standardised scores in Table A, they are the same for both Forms A and B. Table B, on page 69, shows the percentile scores of the actual sample.

Caution is needed when interpreting percentile scores, as they can be confused with percentages. The 30th percentile, for example, is the score (number of words correctly read) which delineates the bottom-performing 30% of pupils from the top 70% in that age group: in other words, 30% of the pupils in this age group scored *below* this score. The 50th percentile is by definition the central score of all the pupils in that age group and corresponds to a standardised score of 100 in Table A: half of the number of pupils in each age group will score below the 50th percentile score and the other half will score above it.

Scores below the 16th percentile are of concern, as they indicate performance that is well below average (see Figure 3.1).

Percentile scores also allow us to compare a pupil's progress relative to other pupils year by year. For example, a pupil who at age 7:0 scores below the 20th percentile (i.e. in the bottom 20% of the group) but when reaching the age of 9:0 scores above the 40th percentile has made definite improvement in reading accuracy relative to his/her peers.

Reading ages

Reading ages are age-equivalent scores that indicate the average score progression of age groups. Note that the reading ages provided by the *DRA* are obtained from the pupil's reading accuracy scores only, and not from the reading comprehension scores.

Although unsuitable for statistical analysis and monitoring purposes, reading ages are very useful when used in a developmental context and helpful in matching a pupil to appropriate reading resources. Development of reading is rapid in the early years of primary school and much slower after age ten. Standardised scores are more appropriate when assessing small increments of change in reading ability, because the pupil's performance is then compared with that of pupils of a similar chronological age group in the standardisation sample of weak readers.

Fluency/reading rate

The process of converting sequences of letters into sequences of sounds may be done consciously and laboriously, or automatically and rapidly. The speed with which words are decoded and read correctly is, therefore, likely to be an indication of how successfully phonic skills have been internalised. There is some evidence that dyslexics have a particular difficulty developing automaticity in skills such as these (e.g. see Nicolson and Fawcett, 1990). This means that, even though their reading may develop to a point where it is accurate, it remains slower and requires more effort than it does for other people. It is, therefore, worthwhile gaining an impression of the speed of reading of the passages – especially those that are read accurately – and recording this on the *Pupil Record*.

Table 3.2 enables you to compare a pupil's fluency/reading rate with that of other pupils of the same *chronological* age. It may also be helpful to use the same table to consider whether the pupil's fluency is broadly in line with his or her *reading* age (see Chapter 5 for further background).

Comprehension measure

Poor comprehension of text may be due to limited 'sight vocabulary', poor phonic skills, or alienation from the task. However, many weak readers can decode and read the words aloud, but still have trouble understanding the complete meaning of the sequence of words that make up the phrase or sentence. The comprehension questions are there to help teachers determine if the reading age (which is based on *accuracy*) is a genuine measure of true reading competence or one that masks a problem of reading with understanding. If a pupil's comprehension score is low, it then becomes important to ascertain whether he or she has a general problem with comprehension of language.

Therefore, a valuable extra feature is incorporated into the *DRA* via the initial *Listening Comprehension* questions. Performance on these questions may be compared to the pupil's performance on the questions following the first reading passage that they meet, where both passage and questions are pitched at the same difficulty level. A discrepancy in performance here may indicate that comprehension difficulties are specific to reading. However, a similar level of difficulty with both sets of questions may suggest an underlying difficulty with aural comprehension.

Table 3.3 enables you to compare a pupil's reading comprehension with other pupils of the same *chronological* age. It may also be helpful to use the same table to consider whether the pupil's comprehension is broadly in line with his or her *reading* age (see *Using the reading comprehension answers* on page 32 for further details)

National Curriculum levels and reading ages

It is important for teachers in many schools in England and Wales to be able to review a pupil's performance against information generated by National Curriculum tests. Table 3.5, based on 280 pupils for whom NC levels were available, indicates a clear pattern or relationship between

Table 3.5: National Curriculum levels of pupils at different Reading Ages

Reading age	\multicolumn{6}{c}{Percentage of pupils at each National Curriculum level}
	Level 1	Level 2	Level 3	Level 4	Level 5	Level 6
<5	28.6	7.6				
5	25.7	17.4	11.1	12.8		
6	25.7	13.0	3.2	2.6		
7	11.4	10.9	4.8	–		
8	5.7	18.5	11.1	–		
9	2.9	15.2	11.1	5.1		
10		10.9	31.7	12.8		
11		2.2	15.9	12.8		
12		3.3	4.8	10.3		
13		–	6.3	15.4	2.4	
14		1.1		7.7	4.8	
15				5.1	11.9	16.7
16				2.6	16.7	16.7
17				5.1	23.8	–
>17				7.7	40.5*	66.7*

* Inflated by a few able readers.

reading ages and National Curriculum levels in English. (In this table, pupils' reading ages have been rounded to the nearest whole number: for example, a pupil at reading age 10:5 has been rounded to 10, while a pupil at 10:6 months has been rounded to 11.) Reference to the table will enable you to assess whether your pupils match the norms obtained in the standardisation or have obtained disparate results for reading compared to performance in written English examinations.

It may be helpful to explore if there is also a link between the *comprehension* score obtained by a pupil from the *DRA* and that pupil's National Curriculum level, as both measure a pupil's ability to comprehend what is written to be able to answer correctly. However, each gathers the answers in a very different manner. Whereas pupils respond orally in the *DRA*, in the National Curriculum tests they write their answers, so their comprehension could be underestimated if their writing skills are not sufficiently developed to enable them to record their understanding.

4 Error analysis: reading accuracy and comprehension

Using reading accuracy information

This chapter describes how reading errors may be used to shed light on the strategies being used by pupils in their reading. It is based on an approach known as *miscue analysis* and has been used widely in the formal and informal assessment of reading. This approach emphasises that reading is an active process, whereby the reader is working to understand the meaning of what is being read. A significant part of the process involves prediction, based on knowledge of grammatical structure and prior experiences, followed by confirmation of those predictions. If the predictions are not confirmed, then re-reading is required to correct either the prediction or the reading itself in order to make sense of the text.

Successful reading depends on the effective use of a range of strategies, including the use of cues from the text to predict unknown or unrecognised words. The National Literacy Strategy (1999 and 2000) represents these cues as a set of searchlights, each of which sheds light on the text. It identifies the searchlights as:

- phonic cues;
- knowledge of context;
- grammatical knowledge;
- word recognition and graphic knowledge.

Fluent readers are adept at using all of these cueing systems and at using them to cross-check the accuracy of their reading. Consequently, when a pupil is struggling with learning to read, it is useful to reflect on which strategies he or she is able to use efficiently and effectively, and which need further development.

Phonic cues

Phonic cues can be used to support the decoding of individual words, especially in the early stages of learning to read, when a child may focus on the initial letter and substitute a word beginning with the same sound, for example reading *cat* instead of *car*. As reading develops, the child learns to take into account all the letters in the word, moving from a focus on the initial letter to taking the final phoneme into consideration and finally incorporating the medial phoneme(s).

Knowledge of context

Readers bring a set of expectations with them when encountering any text. The first such expectation is that the text will make sense. Another is that it will conform, to a greater or lesser extent, to their previous experiences with the particular genre – for example, that a diary entry will be written in the first person and generally in the past tense. Such expectations support reading at two levels: globally and locally. For example, at a global level, pupils with an understanding of the structure of fairy stories may use their contextual knowledge to support decoding of *Once upon a time* . . . .

An example of context supporting decoding at a local level can be found in Non-fiction 3 of Form A of the *DRA*, which comprises instructions for making a cup of tea. One of the sentences reads *Add milk and sugar if you like*. Once the pupil has read the easier words *Add milk and*, the context supports the reading of *sugar* as this is the most likely addition to tea after milk.

Grammatical knowledge

Readers also use grammatical knowledge when attempting to decode unknown words. One unconscious way they do this is by anticipating, for example, whether the word is likely to be an adjective or a verb. A good example of this occurred when a pupil substituted *incredible* for *unreadable* in the following sentence from Fiction 9: *He methodically trawled the room from left to right, front to back, scratching rapid, almost unreadable notes*. Here, one adjective was substituted for another.

Word recognition and graphic knowledge

Readers have a number of words that they recognise by sight. These begin with a child's own name and the high-frequency words taught in the early stages of reading, and develop until adulthood. Fluent readers rarely encounter a word they do not recognise, unless they are reading technical literature from an area with which they are not familiar or texts in historical language, such as Chaucer's *Canterbury Tales*. Partial graphic knowledge is also possible: where a word is recognised just on the basis of one or two of its letters. This may happen particularly when a pupil's reading lexicon, and the entries in it, are not fully developed.

When readers make errors in their reading, the errors can be analysed according to the type of cue that has apparently been used, albeit inefficiently. These attempts provide the teacher with information both about the cues that pupils use when attempting to decode unknown words and, conversely, about those which they may need further encouragement to use. The under-used cueing systems could be modelled for the pupil, for example during shared reading.

However, it is not always possible to identify the specific cue that has been used, as the error could result from the inefficient use of more than one strategy. An example of this occurred where a pupil read *erupted* as *exploded* in the sentence *Two thousand years ago, a volcano erupted in Italy*, in Non-fiction 7. This error could have arisen from the use of phonic cues, context or grammatical knowledge: only through discussion with the pupil might the teacher be able to identify the strategy used. However, examining all the errors made by a reader will often point up a common strategy that is associated with the errors, and this is well worth exploring further.

Some examples

The following examples illustrate the use of the *DRA* with pupils of different ages and reading attainment. While the assessments were being carried out, the administrator noted the errors made by the pupil for later evaluation and categorisation. In every case, the pupil is attempting the most demanding of his or her three reading passages: this is when error analysis is likely to be most informative.

EXAMPLE 4.1
A pupil reading Form B Non-fiction 2 had considerable difficulty, making ten substitutions (Figure 4.1).

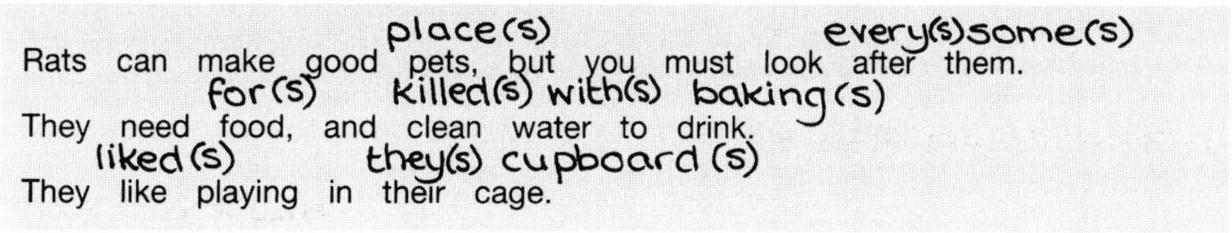

> Rats can make good pets, but you must look after them. [place(s) / every(s) some(s)]
> They need food, and clean water to drink. [for(s) killed(s) with(s) baking(s)]
> They like playing in their cage. [liked(s) they(s) cupboard(s)]

Figure 4.1

Text	Substitution	Cueing strategy
pets	place	phonic, graphic
after	every	
them	some	
food	for	phonic, graphic
clean	killed	phonic
water	with	phonic, graphic
drink	baking	phonic, graphic with b/d reversal?
like	liked	phonic, graphic, contextual, grammatical
their	they	phonic, graphic
cage	cupboard	phonic, graphic, contextual, grammatical

This pupil appears to rely heavily on phonic and graphic information when decoding the text, especially the initial phoneme, and pays little attention to the context. Consequently he is able to gain very little meaning from what he has read – as indicated by his comprehension score of 0 on this passage. This pupil could benefit from being encouraged to consider all the letters in words and also to monitor what he is reading to check that it makes sense.

EXAMPLE 4.2
A pupil reading Form A Non-fiction 3 likewise experienced considerable difficulty with the passage and made a range of errors, comprising a substitution, an omission, two refusals and three insertions (Figure 4.2).

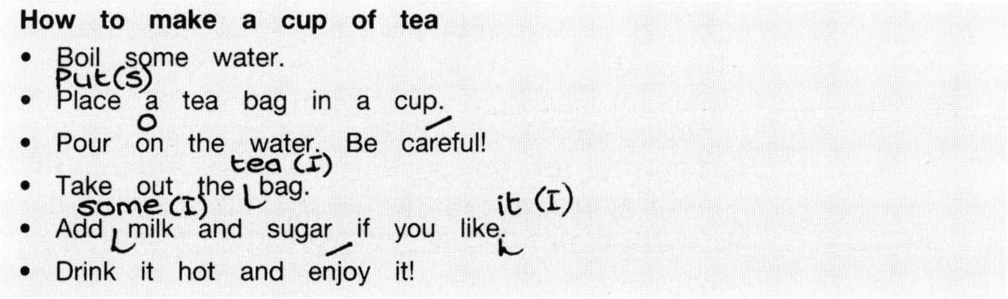

> **How to make a cup of tea**
> - Boil some water.
> - Place a tea bag in a cup. [Put(s) / O]
> - Pour on the water. Be careful!
> - Take out the bag. [tea(I)]
> - Add milk and sugar if you like. [some(I) / it(I)]
> - Drink it hot and enjoy it!

Figure 4.2

Error analysis: reading accuracy and comprehension

The substitution of *Put* for *Place* suggests some use of all the cueing systems, as it:

- fits the context;
- completes the sentence grammatically;
- has the same initial sound and letter as the target word.

Text	Substitution	Cueing strategy
Place	Put	phonic, graphic, contextual, grammatical

The overall sense of meaning was not compromised by either the three insertions (*tea*, *some*, *it*) or by the omission (*on*). As such, concentrating on overall context to encourage a self-correction strategy is unlikely to be beneficial to improving this pupil's reading, but in a follow-up the pupil could be directed to recognise what they are doing. One possibility for a checking strategy is to ensure a one-to-one match between the words on the page and those spoken.

Finally, this pupil was not prepared to attempt the words *careful* and *enjoy*. These refusals may indicate a lack of understanding of morphemes. Further reinforcement of, and practice in, breaking words down into their constituent morphemes might well develop the pupil's confidence in tackling unknown words of this type. Practice activities could be based around identifying 'words within words' (the roots *care* and *joy* in these examples) as well as splitting words into root + suffix (as in *careful*) and prefix + root (as in *enjoy*).

EXAMPLE 4.3

A pupil reading Form B Fiction 4 self-corrected one word and made five substitutions (Figure 4.3).

>   writing (s)   Ran (sc)
> The boys were waiting under a tree. Rain was beginning to fall.
>   boys (s)   left (s)
> The bus had not come and they were going to be late for school.
>   that (s)
> They did not know what to do.
>   Saturday (s)
> Then, suddenly, Tony had a great idea.

Figure 4.3

Text	Substitution	Cueing strategy
waiting	writing	phonic, graphic, grammatical
bus	boys	phonic, graphic, grammatical
late	left	phonic, graphic
what	that	graphic
suddenly	Saturday	phonic, graphic

This pupil appears to use a range of cues, but with too much emphasis placed on graphic and phonic cues, especially the first and last phoneme. It is possible that this pupil would benefit from further practice with vowel digraphs, as a number of the substitutions involve these, as does the self-correction, where *Rain* was originally read as *Ran*.

The first two substitutions are grammatically correct, with the substituted words being from the same word classes as the target words. However, they do not make sense within the context of the passage, so the pupil should be encouraged to monitor what he is reading, checking that he understands the meaning of the text and re-reading sections if necessary.

EXAMPLE 4.4

In the case of a pupil reading Form A Fiction 6, the errors were predominantly substitutions (Figure 4.4). However, the first error was the insertion of two words *in the* into the first sentence: *It was early morning.* There was also one instance where the pupil self-corrected: he initially read *they* for *the* in the sentence *There was sand, as far as the eye could see,* before reading on and encountering *eye*. Both the insertion and the self-correction are syntactically and semantically acceptable alternatives to the actual text.

```
                    in the (I)
It was early ͜ morning. The travellers looked across the
                                        they (sc)
desert. There was sand, as far as the eye could see.
       unexplained (s)             desert (s)
Then, unexpectedly, they heard distant voices. They had

company! Should they be suspicious?
                    were (s)                          raiders (s)
A group of camels was coming towards them, the riders
decided (s) to (s) wait (s)  those (s)
dressed in white. Were these people friends?
```

Figure 4.4

The substitutions were analysed to explore the cues used by the pupil.

Text	Substitution	Cueing strategy
unexpectedly	unexplained	phonic, graphic, contextual
distant	desert	phonic, graphic, contextual
was	were	phonic, grammatical
riders	raiders	phonic, graphic, contextual, grammatical
dressed	decided	phonic, grammatical, graphic
in	to	*These appear to have been triggered by the previous error.*
white	wait	
these	those	phonic, grammatical, graphic

From the analysis, it appears that the pupil is using all the cueing systems in his reading. There does, however, appear to be an over-emphasis on the initial, and to a lesser extent the final, grapheme, and the pupil could perhaps benefit from directing more attention to the graphemes in the middle of words.

EXAMPLE 4.5

A pupil reading Form A Non-fiction 8 began with four omission errors, as he did not read the title of the passage, despite prompting. He also made four substitution errors and one refusal, when no attempt was made to pronounce the word *pressure*. There was one self-correction in this passage as well, as *chemical* was first read as *chemistry* (Figure 4.5).

> **Science on the move**
> ○ ○○ ○
> Science on the move *science fiction (s)*
> These are some of the scientific principles involved in riding a bicycle.
> *effort(s)*
> The helmet shape reduces the effect of air resistance.
> *Chemistry (sc)*
> Chemical ~~energy~~ from food provides the driving force.
> Brakes create friction to slow the wheels down.
> *trays(s)*   *observer(s)*
> Air pressure in the tyres acts as a shock absorber.
> Forces operate the brakes through the action of levers.

Figure 4.5

The substitutions were analysed to explore the cues used by the pupil.

Text	Substitution	Cueing strategy
scientific	science fiction	phonic, graphic
effect	effort	phonic, graphic, grammatical
tyres	trays	phonic, graphic, grammatical
absorber	observer	phonic, graphic, grammatical

From the analysis, it appears that the pupil is using his phonic, graphic and grammatical knowledge but not contextual cues, as the errors are not semantically acceptable alternatives. He needs to be encouraged to check the sense of what he is reading, rather than focusing on each word in isolation. Again, there appears to be an over-emphasis on the initial and final grapheme, and this pupil too could perhaps benefit from directing more attention to the middle grapheme(s).

EXAMPLE 4.6

A pupil reading Form B Fiction 9 made seven substitution errors and one refusal, when no attempt was made to pronounce the word *foreign* (Figure 4.6).

> After just two days in France, I realised that going on holiday with Sam was
> *inspection(s)*   *would(s)*
> a serious mistake. Her insistence that she should always be next to the
> *whining(s)*
> window of the coach, and her constant whingeing about foreign food, were ruining
> *pattern(s)*
> my holiday and exhausting my patience.
> *in(s) instant(s)*   *completed(s)*
> We arrived at an ancient castle, to visit the dungeons. I had not contemplated
> anything vindictive. But as she trudged along, bombarding me with her complaints,
> a cunning plan formed in my mind.

Figure 4.6

The substitutions were analysed to explore the cues used by the pupil.

Text	Substitution	Cueing strategy
insistence	inspection	phonic, graphic, grammatical
should	would	phonic, graphic, grammatical
whingeing	whining	phonic, graphic, grammatical, contextual
patience	pattern	phonic, graphic, grammatical
at	in	grammatical
ancient	instant	grammatical
contemplated	completed	phonic, graphic, grammatical

Every substitution was grammatically correct, as each one was from the same word class as the target word. Five of the seven substitutions could also have been derived using phonic and/or graphic information. However, most of the substitutions were semantically inappropriate, suggesting that the pupil was not monitoring what he was reading and checking that it made sense.

It is possible that the pupil was aware of being timed during this test and was overly concerned with reading at what he felt to be an appropriate pace. If this was thought to be the case, it would be worthwhile asking the pupil to read aloud a passage of comparable difficulty without timing him, to check whether he monitored his reading and corrected errors in this situation.

The reading comprehension questions and answers

The comprehension questions were written to enable teachers and test administrators to determine how effectively pupils have understood what they have read. A number of *types* of question were designed to help give a better picture of the different forms of understanding a pupil is able to gain from a text.

It is possible to categorise the comprehension questions in a variety of ways (see Table 4.1). These include:

Literal probes
These questions may best be described as expecting the pupil to find a word or phrase in the text that will supply the correct answer. In essence, they are simple data matching and/or retrieval exercises.

Inferential or summative probes
These questions require a much higher-order set of skills than those assessing literal recognition. They test to find if the meaning of a 'chunk' of text has been internalised and understood and can be applied to answer the question. These questions require an extra level of understanding, drawing on such skills as evaluation and synthesis. For example, in many cases the information required to answer the question has to be gathered from different places in the text. To be able to undertake this can also require the pupil to know the meaning of the key word or words in the question. These key words are deliberately *not* taken from the text, as this would enable the pupil to work in a literal mode. Many of these questions then require pupils to have a wider listening/speaking or aural vocabulary than written/reading vocabulary.

Predictive probes

These questions require the pupil to make a reasonable suggestion in the light of the information they have read. They are normally associated with fiction rather than non-fiction. They are much more open than the literal questions – and, indeed, many of the inferential and summative questions. As such, the answers may be more wide ranging. Their importance is that they act as a very good check to see if the overall sense and meaning of the story of the passage has been comprehended.

They are usually predicated on something like *What could happen next?*, so they require the concept of time and sequence of events to have been gathered from the passage. They also ask pupils to speculate, which requires an extra measure of self-confidence compared to just responding to task. For weak and very poor readers, these questions may cause consternation, as such pupils will already be at or beyond their personal comfort zones and the questions therefore need to be presented sensitively. Replies such as *Dunno* to predictive questions are indicative of pupils who are struggling, particularly if they have been able to read the words quite successfully.

Vocabulary probes

Some questions test a pupil's ability to understand the meaning of a specific word in context. These types of question only occur in the passages designed for the older age ranges.

Using the reading comprehension answers

By design, the passages in Forms A and B were written to be of similar genres for each level of demand. To help you make use of the comprehension question data, the questions have been categorised against the four probes described above. The analysis of the comprehension questions for Forms A and B in Table 4.1 illustrates how similar the two Forms are and supports the face validity of the test. It shows the two Forms to be extremely close parallels.

In Table 4.1, each question has been placed in only one category: a more sophisticated analysis was found to be more confusing than helpful. Individual experts may well wish to debate some decisions, but for the practical purposes of using the information to help devise successful next-step strategies and inform IEPs, for example, the table is sufficiently detailed.

After the reading test, when reviewing a *Pupil Record*, it is helpful to examine which *types* of question the pupil answered incorrectly or unsatisfactorily. Recording this information on the front of the *Pupil Record* makes for ease of reference on future occasions. An alternative is to record the incorrect questions in the grid supplied by the CD-ROM and this then stores the information for comparison on a future occasion, as well as providing an analysis of the pattern of correct and incorrect answers and comprehension score.

Table 4.1: Analysis of the *DRA* comprehension questions

	Form A				Form B			
	Literal	*Infer-summ*	*Predict*	*Vocab*	*Literal*	*Infer-summ*	*Predict*	*Vocab*
Listening A	1, 3	2	4		1, 3	2	4	
Listening B	1, 2	3	4		1, 2	3	4	
Listening C	1, 3	2, 4	5		1, 3	2, 4	5	
Listening D	1, 2	3, 6	5	4	1, 2	3, 6	5	4
Listening E	1, 2, 5	3, 4, 6	7, 8		1, 2, 5	3, 4, 6	7, 8	
Fiction 2	1, 3	2	4		1, 2	3	4	
Non-fiction 2	1, 2, 3, 4				1, 2, 4	3		
Fiction 3	1, 2	3	4		1, 3	2	4	
Non-fiction 3	1, 2, 3, 4				1, 2, 4		3	
Fiction 4	2, 4	1	3		3	1, 2	4	
Non-fiction 4	1, 2	3, 4			1, 2	3, 4		
Fiction 5	1, 2, 3	4	5		1, 2, 3	4	5	
Non-fiction 5	1, 2, 3, 4	5			1, 3, 4	2, 5		
Fiction 6	1, 3, 4	2	5		2, 3, 4	1	5	
Non-fiction 6	1, 2, 3	5		4	1, 2, 3	5		4
Fiction 7	2, 3, 4	1, 6	5		1, 3, 4	2	5, 6	
Non-fiction 7	2, 3, 5	4, 6		1	1, 2, 4, 5	6		3
Fiction 8	1, 5	2, 3, 4	6		1	2, 4, 5, 6	3	
Non-fiction 8	2, 4, 5	1, 3, 6			2, 4, 5, 6	1, 3		
Fiction 9	1, 2, 3	4	6	5	2, 4	1	3, 6	5
Non-fiction 9	2, 4	1, 3, 6		5	1, 3	2, 4, 5		6
Fiction 10	1, 2, 3, 4	6	7, 8	5	1, 2, 3, 5, 6	7	8	4
Non-fiction 10	1, 2, 4	6, 8	7	3, 5	1, 3, 4	2, 6, 7	8	5
Fiction 11	1, 3, 4, 5	2	7, 8	6	1, 2, 3, 4	6	5, 8	7
Non-fiction 11	2, 3, 4, 8	1, 5, 7		6	1, 2, 4, 6, 7	3, 5		8

Difficulty answering inferential questions

What it may indicate

Inferential questions tend to be harder for most readers than straightforward literal ones. Nevertheless, some pupils will have a noticeable and particular difficulty with making inferences and/or predictions. In extreme cases this may indicate a wider difficulty with language and communication. It may, however, simply indicate that a pupil is unclear about what constitutes a legitimate answer to a question, and feels the text needs to be quoted directly. Such pupils are likely to read back through the text, and offer a chunk of it, or a single word from it, as an answer.

Where pupils are learning English as an additional language, it may show limited background knowledge available to appreciate the cultural references that are often necessary for successful inference. Other pupils also may, for various reasons, have insufficient background knowledge. In particular, a lack of experience with stories will limit an appreciation of story structure, and so make prediction difficult.

The way forward

Where inferential reading comprehension appears to be a particular problem, it should be checked whether a similar pattern is emerging in listening comprehension. If it is, an observation of a pupil's wider language and communication skills is likely to be helpful. For instance, it could be observed whether a pupil:

- has difficulty following instructions in lessons;
- tends to take instructions such as *'Can you sit down now?'* very literally, perhaps by answering *'Yes'* and not sitting down;
- often says things that appear irrelevant to a topic being discussed in a lesson, or to a conversation.

Where this is the case, advice from a speech and language therapist or an educational psychologist should be sought.

Where chunks of text, possibly irrelevant, are being offered as answers, explain to the pupil that you want to know what he or she thinks, and that you want answers in his or her own words. Inferential understanding can be explained to a pupil as a form of detective work, where the text offers small clues that have to be assembled to solve the problem. Some available published materials are designed specifically to develop inferential comprehension.

If the pupil is learning English as an additional language, an enriched and broadened experience with English, both written and spoken, is likely to be helpful in helping him or her read 'between the lines' in texts such as these.

It should be remembered that a proportion of pupils learning English as an additional language will also have wider difficulties with language and communication. Where this is suspected, a language assessment conducted in their first language should be carried out.

Comparing listening comprehension with reading comprehension

A comparison may also be made between the *Listening Comprehension* question score and the first *Reading Comprehension* score.

Listening comprehension higher than reading comprehension

What it may indicate

In such cases, a pupil's comprehension difficulties are likely to be specific to reading and not affect their everyday understanding of spoken language. This may result from inefficient decoding skills, or particularly slow and laboured reading, leading to the meaning being lost along the way. This is often seen in pupils with dyslexia.

However, research studies reviewed in Stothard (1996) suggest that poor reading comprehension, in children whose decoding is satisfactory, results from a variety of difficulties that may also affect their listening comprehension (see below). In general, they read in a very passive manner and fail to monitor their understanding of the text whilst reading.

The way forward

For the dyslexic pupil whose comprehension of text is constrained by poor word level skills, learning support must clearly focus on the development of decoding ability.

However, this should not be at the expense of the all-important text-level skills of using context cues efficiently, as well as drawing on general and linguistic knowledge. These may be potential areas of strength and children sometimes need encouragement or even 'permission' to make use of these other strategies to help themselves.

Reading the 'blurb' on book covers, the chapter headings and the first and last paragraphs in each chapter, as well as looking carefully at the illustrations, are all ways of getting a rough idea of the content before reading a text carefully and can aid 'reading for meaning'.

Whilst reading, pupils should pause now and then to reflect on, and put into their own words, the gist of the sections just read. If they cannot do so, they need strong encouragement to re-read that part – perhaps aloud – and ask themselves *Did that make sense?*

Using inference and prediction can be developed by questions such as *Why do you think that happened?* or *Why do you think she said that?* and *What do you think is going to happen next?*

All these strategies promote active monitoring of meaning whilst reading. *Cloze* exercises can also be used to develop the use of prediction to aid decoding and hence understanding.

Listening comprehension and reading comprehension are both weak

What it may indicate
Research suggests (see Stothard, 1996) that of the one in ten children with *specific* reading *comprehension* difficulties (but age-appropriate reading *accuracy*), most have general language comprehension difficulties. Causal factors include restricted vocabulary, limited verbal reasoning skills, and difficulties with drawing inferences and integrating information from different sources.

The way forward
Substantial support may be needed to help pupils such as these read well for meaning. Approaches include getting a rough idea of the content of a book before reading it, for instance by discussing the 'blurb' on book covers, the chapter headings, and first and last paragraphs in each chapter, as well as looking carefully at the illustrations.

Another approach is to encourage pupils to pause now and then while reading to reflect on, and then put into their own words or visualise, the gist of the sections just read. If they cannot do so, they need strong encouragement to reread that part – perhaps aloud – and ask themselves *Did that make sense?*

Using inference and prediction can be developed by questions such as *Why do you think that happened?* or *Why do you think she said that?* and *What do you think is going to happen next?*

However, remediation should also include work on general language processes – in particular development of vocabulary, since this is crucial to linguistic comprehension and thus to reading comprehension also. A speech and language therapist will be able to offer further advice on developing oral comprehension.

5 Using the *DRA* diagnostically

As well as being used to measure the strength or weakness of a pupil's reading, and to analyse errors in both reading aloud and answering the comprehension questions, the *DRA* may be used to provide more detailed diagnostic information. This can indicate the *type* of any difficulties he or she may be experiencing, what further assessment might be needed and what the focus of any intervention would be.

The *DRA* gives information on four processes:

- reading accuracy
- reading comprehension
- listening comprehension
- fluency/reading rate.

Marked differences between the scores in these processes provide indications of the sorts of barriers to learning to read that a pupil may be encountering.

You are encouraged to record the pupil's errors in word identification, as described in Chapter 4, and to note his or her approach to reading aloud and answering the questions. This qualitative information can also be analysed to show in more detail where difficulties may lie, and used formatively to indicate the way forward. The *photocopiable* **Diagnostic Checklist** (at the end of this Manual) provides a convenient means of bringing all this information together.

Reading processes

Oral accuracy

Accuracy in reading the words in a test such as the *DRA* can perhaps best be thought of as accurate *word recognition in connected, meaningful text*.

When individual words are read *in isolation*, the reader is required to:

- recognise a word immediately on sight;
- and/or recognise it because of its similarity to a word already known;
- and/or recognise the word by decoding it, with or without conscious effort, using correspondences between letters or groups of letters (graphemes) and speech sounds (phonemes) – in other words, to make use of *phonics*.

The process of immediate whole-word recognition on sight is sometimes referred to as a *lexical* process, while that involving phonics is referred to as a *sublexical* process (Coltheart et al, 2001). Recognising a word because it is similar to a word already known is referred to as reading *by analogy* (Goswami, 1994).

There is much evidence that these are also the main processes involved in reading *continuous text*. However, in continuous text, another strategy is also available to help a reader identify a word: an awareness of the grammar (*syntax*) and the meaning (*semantics*) of the text surrounding the word being read – in other words, an awareness of the word's *context*. Research has shown that, at the very least, the use of context can allow the reader to predict aspects of the meaning of an upcoming word, so speeding its recognition, and to select from the alternative meanings of ambiguous words (Adams, 1990).

Indeed, reading is sometimes portrayed as an interaction between word recognition processes and contextual processes (Stanovich, 1980). Good readers are said mostly to recognise words effortlessly, and use context primarily as a check on the accuracy of what they have read. Weaker readers may rely more heavily on the context.

These various influences on accurate word identification in meaningful text are reflected in the National Literacy Strategy's 'searchlight model' (see page 25).

Reading comprehension

Successful reading comprehension is the main purpose of reading. It can be thought of as being primarily dependent on two overarching abilities (Stuart, 2003):

- word recognition
- general language comprehension.

These can be represented as shown in Figure 5.1, further details of which can be accessed at
www.standards.dfee.gov.uk/pdf/ literacy/mstuart_phonics

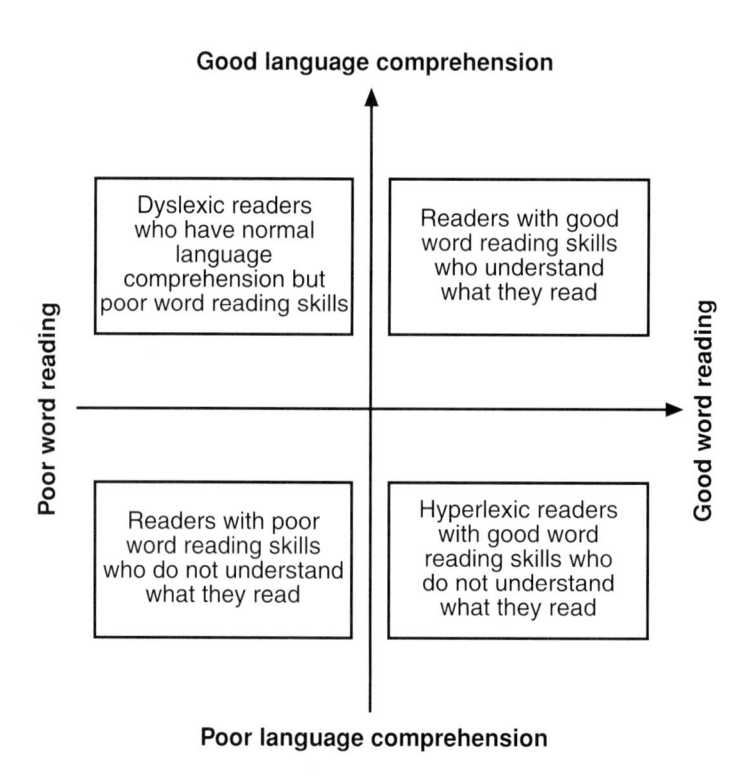

```
                    Good language comprehension
                                 ▲
         ┌──────────────────┐    │    ┌──────────────────┐
         │ Dyslexic readers │    │    │ Readers with good│
         │ who have normal  │    │    │ word reading     │
         │ language         │    │    │ skills who       │
         │ comprehension but│    │    │ understand       │
         │ poor word reading│    │    │ what they read   │
         │ skills           │    │    │                  │
         └──────────────────┘    │    └──────────────────┘
  Poor                           │                          Good
  word ──────────────────────────┼──────────────────────────► word
  reading                        │                           reading
         ┌──────────────────┐    │    ┌──────────────────┐
         │ Readers with poor│    │    │ Hyperlexic       │
         │ word reading     │    │    │ readers with good│
         │ skills who do not│    │    │ word reading     │
         │ understand what  │    │    │ skills who do not│
         │ they read        │    │    │ understand what  │
         │                  │    │    │ they read        │
         └──────────────────┘    │    └──────────────────┘
                                 ▼
                    Poor language comprehension
```

Figure 5.1 (after Stuart, 2003)

A high degree of success in word identification is necessary for reading comprehension, but it is not enough by itself. Comprehension of language in general is required too: the *DRA*'s listening comprehension passages provide a pointer here. So, in the diagram opposite, pupils who are good at reading comprehension will be in the top right-hand quarter, as both of the contributory skills are good. Those dyslexic pupils whose oral comprehension skills are good will be in the top left-hand corner, indicating the particular difficulty they face with word-level aspects of reading.

Poor language comprehension may itself also have an impact on the development of word identification, especially as a pupil becomes older. Semantic context will be less helpful in determining the meaning of words not previously encountered, and so limit the broadening of a pupil's reading vocabulary (Snowling, 2002).

A wide variety of skills are needed to understand text adequately (Oakhill and Yuill, 2002). Among these are:

- ability to make inferences
- understanding text structure
- comprehension monitoring.

The ability to make inferences – to 'read between the lines' – is especially important, allowing readers to go beyond what is explicitly stated in text. The *DRA* is designed to assess inferential as well as literal understanding of the text. The ability to predict what will happen, for instance in a story that is left hanging, depends heavily on the ability to make inferences, and also draws on an understanding of text structure. Table 4.1, on page 33, shows which questions in the *DRA* are of which type.

Lack of comprehension monitoring can be observed during oral reading, for instance when a pupil appears not to notice when what he or she has read does not make sense. Self-correction, especially when it occurs some way 'downstream' of a reading error, may be taken as a sign that meaning is being monitored.

Fluency/reading rate

Fluency is the ability to 'read a text quickly, accurately and with proper expression' (Samuels et al, 2000). Some children who have struggled to learn to read are helped to become accurate in their reading and become adequate comprehenders. However, they may, in spite of this, not be fully fluent readers (Torgeson, 2002). One of the main ways reading fluency is measured is through speed of reading. Age-related norms are given for reading speed in the *DRA*. Fluency may also be gauged more impressionistically by noting, for instance, how often and for how long a pupil hesitates while reading a text, and whether his or her intonation is appropriate to the meaning and grammar of what is being read.

Lack of fluency may be related to a limited 'sight vocabulary', to a lack of automaticity in the underlying reading processes (for instance if the use of phonics remains a conscious process), or to a more general limitation in speed of processing (Wolf and O'Brien, 2001). Visual factors may also affect reading fluency (Evans, 2001; Wilkins et al, 2001).

Reading difficulty, dyslexia and specific learning difficulties

Pupils may have difficulty in successfully developing any of the above processes. A particular difficulty with developing the word-level skills of immediate word recognition and phonics is commonly encountered, and is typical of *dyslexia*.

The current British Psychological Society (1999) working definition of dyslexia states that:

'Dyslexia is evident when accurate and fluent word reading and/or spelling develops very incompletely or with great difficulty. This focuses on literacy learning at the "word level" and implies that the problem is severe and persistent despite appropriate learning opportunities ...'

This is the definition followed in this Manual. It is linked to a view that dyslexia can be identified by comparing reading comprehension with listening comprehension – the difference between the two reflecting word level reading ability. Other views of dyslexia emphasise a discrepancy between general ability and reading attainment, or highlight underlying difficulties with phonological processing.[1] Where such features are indicated by a pupil's performance, they may be taken as further confirmation that dyslexia may be present.

Patterns of results and errors in the *DRA* typical of dyslexia are discussed in the analyses below. However, a formal identification of dyslexia should be based on a wide range of assessments and should be carried out by an educational psychologist or a suitably qualified specialist teacher. The *DRA* can form a valuable part of this process, especially as an initial assessment to provide pointers as to what further assessments would be useful.

Hyperlexia refers to instances of advanced word-recognition skills accompanied by very weak comprehension. It is likely to indicate wider semantic and pragmatic difficulties, and may be associated with autistic spectrum disorders (Nation, 1999). The *DRA* can give an early suggestion of this but, as with dyslexia, more extensive assessment by specialists in the area will need to be carried out.

Analysing performance

The following sections describe some common patterns that will be familiar to experienced users of oral reading tests. Suggestions are offered on what the patterns may mean and how best to proceed.

It must be remembered, nevertheless, that a test such as this only offers a snapshot of a pupil's reading performance. All tests acknowledge that

---

[1] The definition of dyslexia as a discrepancy between general intelligence and reading attainment is now much less widely held than it was previously. For the issues discussed here, see Stanovich (1991) and Stanovich (1998).

pupil performance may vary from one day to the next, and no test that involves the reading of meaningful text can be completely free from cultural bias or other factors that may affect how a pupil carries out the task.

It is important, therefore, where there is concern about a pupil's reading, to carry out further, more detailed assessments. This may involve:

- further standardised tests of reading, such as a reading comprehension test or a test of words, including non-words, read in isolation;
- other standardised tests of, for instance, spelling, phonological awareness or short-term memory;
- qualitative analysis of reading and spelling – for instance, to check exactly which common words are recognised immediately on sight, or what aspects of phonics the pupil is secure in;
- observation of how a pupil undertakes literacy tasks in day-to-day work;
- discussion with the pupil about, for instance, his or her reading habits, likes and dislikes in reading material, or conscious reading strategies;
- discussion with parents, teachers and other relevant adults.

The use of the *DRA* diagnostically can act as a doorway into this process of further assessment, indicating which aspects of reading it would be fruitful to explore in more depth.

The first section below examines what variations between the scores obtained on the *DRA* might mean. The following section examines *qualitative* differences in reading performance. This is mostly concerned with how words are misread, but also takes into account which words are read accurately and observations of the manner in which a pupil is reading.

Analysing patterns in scores

1. A pupil's reading accuracy and reading comprehension scores are both low.

EXAMPLE 5.1

Chronological age	Accuracy Reading Age	Reading Comprehension
10 years 3 months	7 years 6 months	Well below average

What it may indicate
This may mean that word identification ability and general language comprehension are both weak, in which case a pupil such as this is likely to have considerable difficulties developing his or her literacy.

However, it could also mean that, as the pupil's energies were being devoted so much to the difficult process of word identification, the resources available for comprehension were limited.

The major difficulty with reading at the word level may be an indication that this pupil is dyslexic, although other possible reasons for poor reading, such as lack of schooling, need to be considered.

The way forward
The listening comprehension passages should be used to explore whether the low reading comprehension score is primarily a result of limitations in word-level reading or is indicative of wider comprehension difficulties. If wider comprehension difficulties are apparent, a speech and language therapist should be consulted.

An analysis of the oral reading errors should be undertaken to see which sort of words the pupil is finding difficult. This should give an impression of what the focus of the word-level elements of an intervention should be and at what level to start, although supplementary assessments, such as a non-word reading test or checking which NLS sight words the pupil can read, may be necessary. An intervention programme should incorporate techniques and materials that specifically address the development of reading comprehension.

If the word-level difficulties are severe, a fuller assessment should be carried out, where background information, such as history of schooling, is reviewed and underlying factors considered. This may entail assessing phonological awareness and processing, arranging for a hearing test, and requesting a detailed examination from an optometrist.

The school will need to make arrangements to ensure the pupil has as much access as possible to the curriculum in spite of having difficulty accessing written language. Information may need to be presented to him or her through means other than the written word.

2. A pupil's reading accuracy score is low, but his or her reading comprehension score is higher.

EXAMPLE 5.2

Chronological age	Accuracy Reading Age	Reading Comprehension
10 years 3 months	7 years 6 months	Average

What it may indicate
This shows a particular difficulty with word identification, and so difficulty with reading at the word level. This is therefore an indication that this pupil may be dyslexic, although other possible reasons for poor word-level skills, such as lack of schooling, need to be considered.

Dyslexic pupils may have average or good general comprehension which allows them to obtain more meaning from the text than might be expected from their word-identification skills, as appears to be the case here. These strengths do provide them with compensatory strategies, but the word-level limitations can lead to frustration.

The way forward
An analysis of the oral reading errors should be undertaken to see which sort of words the pupil is finding difficult. This should give an impression of what the focus of an intervention should be and at what level to start, although supplementary assessments, such as a non-word reading test or checking which NLS sight words the pupil can read, may be necessary.

If the word-level difficulties are severe, a fuller assessment should be carried out, where background information, such as history of schooling, is reviewed and underlying factors considered. This may entail assessing phonological awareness and processing, arranging for a hearing test, and requesting a detailed examination from an optometrist.

The school will need to make arrangements to ensure the pupil has full access to the curriculum in spite of having difficulty accessing written language. Information may need to be presented to him or her through means other than the written word.

The comparative strength in comprehension is a positive feature, and this should be made clear to the pupil, as strengths such as these can easily be overlooked in a generally weak reading performance. It is likely to be reflected in adequate listening comprehension scores, and it may be useful to confirm, by undertaking verbal and/or non-verbal reasoning tests, that difficulties with the word-level aspects of literacy are specific.

3. A pupil's reading comprehension score is low, but his or her reading accuracy score is higher.

EXAMPLE 5.3

Chronological age	Accuracy Reading Age	Reading Comprehension
10 years 3 months	9 years 5 months	Well below average

What it may indicate
This strongly suggests a difficulty with wider aspects of comprehension than just reading comprehension. In extreme cases, it may indicate hyperlexia and be linked to language and communication disorders.

However, there will be some cases where pupils have the ability to understand written language, but are so concerned to give an accurate oral performance on this test that they do not fully engage with the meaning of what they have read.

There will also be instances of pupils learning English as an additional language whose oral reading skills have outstripped their understanding of the words, structures and social references in the text. There may also be pupils who do not appreciate that the primary purpose in reading English is the extraction of meaning.

The way forward
The listening comprehension passages should be used to explore whether the pupil also has difficulty understanding spoken language.

Where this is the case, advice from a speech and language therapist or an educational psychologist should be sought. An intervention programme should incorporate techniques and materials that directly address the development of reading comprehension, as well as approaches to addressing spoken language and communication needs. Particular care needs to be taken in the classroom to ensure the pupil has followed and understood instructions.

Where a pupil is learning English as an additional language, an enriched, broadened and more intensive engagement with English is indicated.

Depending on how long the pupil has been learning English, the comparatively good oral performance in the absence of full understanding may be a considerable achievement, and should be acknowledged.

Where listening comprehension appears to be adequate, a silent comprehension test can be administered to see whether the pressure to perform orally has hindered comprehension on the *DRA*.

4. A pupil's fluency/reading rate is low, but his or her accuracy and/or comprehension scores are higher.

EXAMPLE 5.4

Chronological age	Accuracy Reading Age	Reading Comprehension	Fluency/ Reading Rate
10 years 3 months	9 years 8 months	Average	Well below average

What it may indicate
This suggests that to some extent word identification does not involve immediate recognition of words and/or that phonic processes are not automatic.

The way forward
An initial step is to observe *how* the pupil is reading the text (see *Analysing patterns of oral errors*, below).

Depending on what is observed, increasing fluency may involve:

- ensuring important common words are recognised immediately on sight by repeated reading of them in isolation, perhaps using flashcards or games. The focus should not just be on accuracy but also on speed of recognition;

- re-reading books or other material to the point where the reading is quick and fluent. This process is best supported and modelled by a fluent reader (adult or peer), and ideally should be for a specific purpose (for instance, reading to a younger child, recording onto tape, reading a play to an audience). *Paired Reading* (see Topping, 1995) is an excellent way of promoting reading fluency and confidence. The method can be taught to parents as well as classroom assistants and other helpers. For maximum benefit, a little reading practice, supported in this way, should take place every day for an initial period of six weeks.

- helping phonic processes to become automatic through reinforcement and 'overlearning' by linking spelling tuition with reading support.

Where reading speed is slow even where accuracy is adequate, pupils are likely to require extra time in public tests and examinations. This can be investigated further using a timed test of reading comprehension, such as one of the *Edinburgh Reading Test* series.

Analysing patterns of oral errors

Important information can be obtained through making an exact running record of any errors in oral reading, and recording other features such as hesitation, self-correction, ignoring of punctuation and appropriateness of intonation. An impression can then be gained of what aspects of oral reading a pupil finds difficult. A focus on whether phonics is being used to attempt unknown words and whether common irregular words[2] are misread can be particularly fruitful, as this gives insight into lexical and sub-lexical processes.

You may find it helpful to summarise the oral errors a pupil makes, together with some of the words read accurately, and make a brief comment on each. Patterns then often quickly emerge in the *analysis* column.

Example 5.5 shows how this may done for one of the early passages of the *DRA*. Example 5.6 illustrates the same process in a more demanding passage.

EXAMPLE 5.5

Word	Read as	Analysis
Sunday	✓	Sounded out and decoded – good use of phonics
football	✓	Recognised immediately
brother	*bother*	Not part of sight vocabulary. Tried to sound out and blend, but omitted second letter in consonant cluster. Does not make sense in context.
tried	*tied*	Omitted second letter in consonant cluster
hard	*h-a-r-d* (blended as *had*)	Not part of sight vocabulary. Good phonic attempt, taking this into account. Digraph 'ar' not known.
over	*over* with 'short o' – then self-corrected when end of sentence reached	Not part of sight vocabulary. Good phonic attempt. Shows *can* use context as a means of checking accuracy.
was	*was* (to rhyme with *gas*)	Not part of sight vocabulary, but very common word. Good phonic attempt. Resulted in non-word that could not make sense in context.
	It is clear this pupil's phonics skills are already developed to some extent, and that this is a strategy he relies on, although he finds consonant clusters difficult and his knowledge of vowel digraphs needs to be developed. His sight vocabulary seems very limited, although he is able to recognise at least one word beyond very basic words immediately on sight – although this may be a word that has particular importance to him. He does not seem too concerned that what he reads does not make sense, but has shown he is not completely unaware of sentence context and is able to use it to correct himself.	

---

[2] Irregular words are words which cannot be decoded solely using grapheme-phoneme conversion rules (phonics). The borderline between regular and irregular words is a shifting one, depending on which grapheme–phoneme conversion rules are taught and which have been internalised by a pupil. Examples of words in the *DRA* that are likely to be irregular for most pupils are: *coming, water, move, brought*. Examples of regular words are: *can, pets, like, strip, assembly*.

EXAMPLE 5.6

Word	Read as	Analysis
Carla's	Carol's	Read without pausing – didn't seem to try to decode
perched	Refused – said 'don't know that one'	
nervously	✓	Recognised at once
branch	✓	Recognised at once
descend	'dez ... that's end – don't know'	Seemed to recognise small words in the longer word
rescue	✓	Recognised at once
attempted	'at... don't know'	Repeated 'A rescue was ...' twice before refusing word – trying to use context. No sign of attempting to decode – recognised *at* at start of word immediately.
disappeared	✓	Recognised at once
Lance	laugh	Using first letter. She had laughed at previous sentence and pointed at picture, which may have influenced choice.
received	recovered	Awareness of *re-* prefix and *-ed* suffix
present	parents	Visually similar. Makes sense in context (but changes meaning and spoils joke)

The pattern that quickly emerges here is of a pupil using very little phonics at all. She relies mainly on recognising a word at once with support from the surrounding context. When she doesn't recognise a word immediately, she may consciously use the context (for instance by taking another run up at *attempted*) or look for words in words – neither strategy appearing to be very successful. She clearly recognises and takes account of some common prefixes and suffixes, such as *re-*, *-ed*, and *'s*. Overall, this results in rather patchy reading, with some apparently difficult words (*nervously, disappeared*) read more easily than some simpler ones (*Carla's, perched, present*). Not having a phonics strategy to fall back on makes her reading appear slapdash and careless, as the best she can do is to guess and to read quickly to maintain the meaning.

Experienced users will find that patterns of this sort may become clear through a simple scrutiny of the *Pupil Record*.

The following suggestions relate to pupils who have obtained low scores for reading accuracy, and for whom more information is required.

1. Struggles with reading both simple regular words and common irregular words.

What it may indicate
It is important to establish what instruction the pupil has received previously, and whether substantial amounts of schooling have been missed.

If there has been previous appropriate teaching, then the pattern indicates a severe general difficulty with reading at the word level, and combines features of 1 and 2 above, namely difficulty with both learning basic phonics and with developing a 'sight vocabulary'. This is likely to point to underlying phonological processing difficulties, possibly combined with other factors. Dyslexic-type difficulties such as these are sometimes referred to as *mixed*.

The way forward
If there have not been previous suitable learning opportunities for the pupil, then the early stages of a general literacy programme, such as the NLS, can be followed and progress in many cases is likely to be rapid.

Where there has been a history of suitable teaching, then a carefully structured programme will need to be implemented, combining the systematic teaching of phonics, the development of a sight vocabulary containing common, probably irregular, words to be recognised at speed, and reading for meaning. Individual targets in each of these areas could be identified. Considerable reinforcement is likely to be necessary, and pupil motivation and self-esteem will need to be monitored and addressed. Multi-sensory techniques that employ and link the visual, auditory and kinaesthetic (movement) senses are likely to be helpful.

A more thorough test of the pupil's phonological abilities may be helpful. Where wider linguistic difficulties are suspected, refer to a speech and language therapist. Parents/carers should be asked whether there is a history of hearing difficulties, such as glue ear. Regular hearing tests should be arranged. A thorough assessment of the pupil's eyesight and visual processing by an optometrist should be arranged, and any treatment or advice given should be followed.

2. Struggles with decoding many regular words, but reads common irregular words more quickly and accurately.

What it may indicate
This suggests weak phonics, but better word recognition. It appears to be a common pattern amongst dyslexic pupils, is likely to indicate weak underlying phonological processing, and, when confirmed by more detailed assessment, is sometimes referred to as *phonological dyslexia*. The relatively better word recognition (sight word) ability may allow the pupil to make some progress with reading on his/her own, but attempting unfamiliar words will remain very difficult. Spelling is likely to remain weak. Weak phonological processing may be a subtle difficulty on its own, or may be a sign of wider speech and language, and/or hearing, difficulties.

The way forward
It is important to establish which grapheme–phoneme (letter–sound) correspondences are known, and whether the pupil is able to blend phonemes to form words. The learning and reinforcement of unfamiliar or only partially known grapheme–phoneme correspondences, and the development of blending skills, would form the basis of individual targets. A programme to achieve these would need to be well-structured and involve considerable reinforcement of what is being learnt.

A more thorough test of the pupil's underlying phonological abilities is likely to be helpful. Where wider linguistic difficulties are suspected, refer to a speech and language therapist. Parents/carers should be asked whether there is a history of hearing difficulties, such as 'glue ear'. Regular hearing tests should be arranged.

3. Decodes uncommon regular words successfully, but unsuccessfully attempts to use phonics also to read common irregular words. Reading slow and laborious.

What it may indicate

This suggests weak instant word recognition, but better phonics. The better phonics may indicate a strength in this area or substantial instruction, and the pupil is relying heavily on it for word identification. This pattern of strength and weakness is sometimes referred to as *surface dyslexia* and is thought to be less common than that found in *phonological dyslexia*. Explanations for it vary, and include underexposure to print (perhaps because of mild phonological difficulties), visual processing, memory or imaging problems, and difficulty with speed of processing, as shown in tests of 'rapid automatic naming'.

The way forward

The amount of reading a pupil such as this does should be increased. Re-reading familiar books may be helpful, with the emphasis on improving speed and intonation. A record can be kept of the number of words read per minute, to monitor whether fluency is increasing. Common, preferably irregular words, that he/she cannot currently read, should be identified and practised on their own, perhaps using flashcards or games, and linking the recognition of the word to its meaning. The focus should not just be on accuracy but also on speed of recognition. The comparative strength with phonics should continue to be developed, with particular attention paid to helping the processes become rapid and automatic. All of these elements of a programme could form the basis of individual targets.

A thorough assessment of the pupil's eyesight and visual processing by an optometrist should be arranged, and any treatment or advice given should be followed.

4. Sounds out letters aloud successfully, but often cannot combine to form real words.

What it may indicate

This shows that grapheme–phoneme correspondences have been learnt, but that there is a particular difficulty with blending, and probably with phonological awareness and processing more generally. The ability to blend is essential for phonic skills in reading to develop. Some children who have struggled with this process find it difficult to then move on to processing common letter strings automatically and persist in sounding out all the letters in a word individually, e.g. /s/l/e/e/p/ for *sleep*; /n/i/g/h/t for *night*.

The way forward

Blending needs to be taught as soon as possible, possibly as part of a structured phonological awareness programme. It needs to be taught alongside, and linked to, letter knowledge and basic reading. Moveable letters, spaced far apart when the phonemes are said separately and then moved together when they are blended, can be a useful resource.

A more thorough test of the pupil's phonological abilities may be helpful. Where wider linguistic difficulties are suspected, refer to a speech and language therapist. Parents/carers should be asked whether there is a history of hearing difficulties, such as glue ear.

For the letter-by-letter reader, recognition of common letter strings – consonant digraphs and blends, vowel digraphs, high-frequency rimes and common prefixes and suffixes – will develop through an integrated spelling and reading programme of instruction. A detailed diagnosis of the pupil's needs in this respect can be obtained via assessment with the *Nonword Reading Test* (Crumpler and McCarty, 2004).

5. Many errors make sense in context, but only one or two letters correspond to the actual word.

What it may indicate
This suggests a difficulty with reading at the word level, as described in 1 to 3 above, but combined with an ability to use context to aid word identification. This is likely to indicate that this pupil reads for meaning, or is at least conscious of the syntactic structures of sentences. These are positive features of his/her reading. However, using context extensively to compensate for weakness at the word level may actually hinder the development of word-level skills, in that it encourages guessing rather than identification based on the actual sequence of letters in words. Phonics and context need to be used in conjunction to allow the learning of new vocabulary through reading.

Nevertheless, the use of context does show some proficiency at the word level, as some words do need to be recognised to provide the context for identifying further words.

The way forward
Good readers do use context to some extent to form expectations of the meaning of upcoming words and to monitor the accuracy of what they have read. The use of context in general terms, therefore, should not be discouraged. Rather, word-level skills should be developed, as described in 1 to 3 above, and their use encouraged when reading continuous text. This may well require pupils' reading to become slower for a while, as they develop a habit of using full 'within word' cues as well as ensuring the word makes sense in context.

6. Errors often result in non-words. Where they result in real words, they are unrelated to the context.

What it may indicate
This suggests that this pupil is reading in a highly mechanistic manner, and does not realise that obtaining meaning is the primary purpose of reading. It may be that phonics instruction has been carried out in isolation and not linked to the meaning of words or texts, or that the pupil has phonological or rote learning strengths, but semantic weaknesses.

The way forward
The teaching strategies used previously should be investigated, and broadened if necessary. Where letters are sounded out and then blended to form words as part of phonics instruction, the pupil should be

encouraged to give the meaning of the resulting words or put them in a sentence. When reading continuous text, the pupil should be encouraged to think of whether a sentence makes sense or 'sounds right', and, if not, to re-read it. It is likely that wider comprehension strategies will need to be taught. The pupil's understanding of spoken language should be checked, perhaps through a listening comprehension test, and semantic aspects of his or her own language considered. Where a general weakness with semantic aspects of language is suspected, advice from a speech and language therapist should be sought.

7. Omits or confuses simple common words that *are* in his/her reading vocabulary, but successfully reads more complex words.

What it may indicate
Although quite commonly observed, there is no agreed explanation of this. Some suggestions are:

- visual processing difficulties are making small words difficult to distinguish from each other;
- fixations[3] are too far apart, so that information from between the fixations is not being properly processed;
- the pupil is paying insufficient attention to the small words because he/she is devoting available resources to identifying more difficult words;
- the pupil confused the small words when he/she was first learning to read and this reappears when reading at speed.

The way forward
It is important to encourage the pupil to monitor the meaning of what he/she is reading so that corrections of these slips where they do affect the meaning can be made. A note can be made of these slips when reading books to see whether a particular pattern emerges – for instance whether specific words are confused (such as *of* and *for*) and the pupil could be encouraged to pay particular attention to these. Slowing down the pupil's reading, at least for a while, and/or encouraging the use of a finger, pencil or other tracking aid may be helpful.

A thorough assessment of the pupil's eyesight and visual processing by an optometrist should be arranged, and any treatment or advice given should be followed. Electronic eye-tracking devices are increasingly available which could determine whether fixations are especially far apart or otherwise unusual.

---

[3] The series of points on a line of text where the eyes rest briefly to take in information. The eyes can usually take in about 9 characters at a time.

8. Gives up quickly on words that he/she does not recognise at once. Does not attempt longer words at all. A high proportion of refusal errors to substitution errors.

What it may indicate
This may suggest the pupil has very limited strategies, either phonic or contextual, available for attempting words that are not immediately familiar. It also suggests he/she has become discouraged and alienated from the task, and may indicate wider issues relating to self-esteem.

The way forward
Check whether this is a general approach of the pupil, or only applies when he/she is tackling more difficult texts. Ensure that material the pupil is being asked to read to develop his or her reading (at school and at home) is not at 'frustrational' level (more than about 1 mistake in 10 words), and if necessary spend time reading books that are easy enough to ensure success.

Strategies to help identify unknown words should be discussed, and phonics developed to a level that makes the use of phonic strategies worthwhile. Ensure that adults listening to the pupil reading know which words the pupil is capable of attempting (in which case they should encourage him/her to attempt them) and which words he/she is not capable of attempting (in which case they should supply the word quickly). Material should be motivating so that the pupil has a reason for trying to work out what the words are. Adults should show pleasure in the books and pleasure when the pupil reads words successfully, so that reading becomes established as a pleasurable activity.

6 Technical information

Standardisation of the DRA

A total of 1600 Form A tests were sent to over 100 schools across England, Wales and Northern Ireland at the beginning of January 2004, for standardisation in January and February 2004. Close to 1200 Form B were supplied in March for the second phase of the standardisation in March and April 2004.

When standardising most reading tests, the researchers use samples distributed across the full ability range, with the majority of pupils around the median of the range. However, *individual* reading tests are normally conducted with pupils who are weaker readers. Accordingly, the majority of the pupils who took part in the standardisation were chosen from the bottom quartile of the reading ability range. The *DRA* standardisation sample was therefore more representative of the pupils the test was actually designed for, rather than a general school population with few individuals in the actual range of interest.

Given the significant bias of the sample, the usual practice of generating age-standardised scores would not be appropriate. For this reason a specialised procedure was adopted, namely to *equate* the standards of the standardisation sample to the results the pupils gained when they took a recently published group reading test, which had itself been standardised with 4000+ pupils. Equating also enabled reliable use of a smaller sample than in conventional standardisations.

The equating was undertaken in the first phase of the standardisation. The pupils in the sample took one of the following calibration tests as well as *DRA* Form A:

- in Years 2–6 (ages 6–11) *Hodder Group Reading Test 2*;
- in Years 7 and 8 (ages 12–13) *Hodder Group Reading Test 3*;
- in Years 9–11 (ages 14–16) *Edinburgh Reading Test 4*.

Taking both *DRA* and a calibration test enabled standards to be equated to norms from large samples of pupils drawn from a normal distribution of the school population. Details of the sample are given in Table 6.1.

For Form A, approximately 1600 *Pupil Record* sheets and group reading tests were distributed to well over 100 schools, Pupil Referral Units, County SEN Support Services and Dyslexia Associations. Many of these are listed in the acknowledgements. In the second phase, some 1200 Form B *Pupil Record* sheets were distributed, together with the *Nonword Reading Test* that was also being standardised at the same time.

As in all trials, a number of the people involved were unable to fulfil their original intentions – for reasons that are many and varied, but not least because the total time commitment, for administering both Forms plus

Table 6.1: The standardisation sample

Age group	Form A Boys	Form A Girls	Form A Total	Form B Boys	Form B Girls	Form B Total
6:6–7:5	7	13	20	5	8	13
7:6–7:11	23	23	46	17	22	39
8:0–8:5	20	21	41	14	16	30
8:6–8:11	22	16	38	14	11	25
9:0–9:5	20	8	28	17	6	23
9:6–9:11	48	19	67	34	14	48
10:0–10:5	27	16	43	22	13	35
10:6–10:11	35	19	54	27	16	43
11:0–11:5	30	22	52	22	14	36
11:6–11:11	16	13	29	16	8	24
12:0–12:5	17	7	24	14	5	19
12:6–12:11	13	8	21	8	7	15
13:0–13:5	32	10	42	22	9	31
13:6–13:11	19	12	31	16	4	20
14:0–14:5	18	10	28	14	8	22
14:6–14:11	11	5	16	10	4	14
15:0–15:5	11	4	15	7	3	10
15:6–15:11	17	6	23	11	5	16
16:0–16:5	12	3	15	9	2	11
Total	*398*	*235*	*633*	*299*	*175*	*474*

the equating test, was significant. To those hard-pressed teachers, peripatetic support workers and teaching assistants who did manage to do all of this we are indebted, as it has enabled us to provide secure information, which we believe those working with low achievers will appreciate when using the *DRA* to assess and assist the reading progress of their pupils.

Teachers and teaching assistants timed the pupils' reading and checked on the understanding of what was read using the comprehension questions. The data to establish the patterns of performance for fluency/reading rate and comprehension could be amalgamated for the first and second phases of the standardisation to provide a sample of over 1100 pupils. It was also possible to examine the test-retest performance of the pupils to obtain a measure of the reliability of the *DRA* (see below).

To ensure that the standardisation was as close as possible to the real-use situation, the reading booklets used were produced in full colour. Prior to the standardisation, small-scale trials had been undertaken in two comprehensive schools, one primary school and across a County SEN Support Service. Advice gained from this stage, together with quality assurance meetings with the authors of the passages, ensured that no subsequent changes were required to the reading passages.

A small number of extra acceptable answers to the comprehension questions were added to the *Pupil Records*, as comments from the teachers and teaching assistants in the standardisation suggested about twenty additional answers that were useful to include. These additions do not affect the data on the comprehension measure, as the teachers indicated that in most cases they had scored the answer as correct, and the extra information will help those administering the tests have a better feel for what is or is not an acceptable response.

Table 6.2 shows the mean (average) and standard deviation of the number of words correctly read for pupils who did both the Form A and B tests, by age.

Table 6.2: Means and standard deviations of words correctly read, for Forms A and B, by age group

Age group	Form A Mean	Form A SD	Form B Mean	Form B SD
6:6–7:5	104.8	29.3	121.2	54.1
7:6–7:11	120.0	25.7	126.7	31.2
8:0–8:5	118.6	21.9	126.4	38.4
8:6–8:11	132.4	45.4	132.8	38.1
9:0–9:5	121.1	29.5	122.1	33.4
9:6–9:11	136.1	37.2	149.4	50.7
10:0–10:5	145.7	43.6	151.5	47.4
10:6–10:11	162.4	59.1	164.6	56.3
11:0–11:5	168.9	60.1	175.0	64.1
11:6–11:11	192.6	58.6	207.3	66.2
12:0–12:5	183.8	54.9	191.9	61.2
12:6–12:11	203.2	66.8	212.1	66.8
13:0–13:5	228.7	61.3	239.3	65.0
13:6–13:11	234.0	61.6	253.4	54.4
14:0–14:5	234.4	55.0	255.6	51.6
14:6–14:11	269.2	41.1	274.3	24.7
15:0–15:5	238.3	67.4	256.8	42.0
15:6–15:11	249.9	60.8	257.4	60.5
16:0–16:5	273.4	40.4	280.5	23.8
All	*172.1*	*68.3*	*180.9*	*71.5*

The Form B tests were designed and trialled to ensure that they had the same demand as the equivalent Form A tests. The differentials in performances between Form A and Form B apparent in the table may be attributed to:

- a 'learning effect' where pupils' reading performance may well have improved naturally during the time interval between taking Form A and Form B;
- a 'test experience' or practice effect where pupils' experience in taking the Form A tests has improved their performance in the Form B tests.

A fallback in performance is quite noticeable at the age group 12:0–12:5 (see below). Other apparent discrepancies in mean values at several places in the table are possibly due to different combinations of the *DRA* reading passages (having different combinations of maximum possible marks) that were taken by these pupils, and other sampling-related variations. The overall picture, however, is as one would expect: a steady improvement in reading ability with age.

The graphs in Figure 6.1 indicate how performance on the different groups of three-passage tests in the standardisation increased as pupils'

Linear equating
Standardised score by accuracy, by age groups

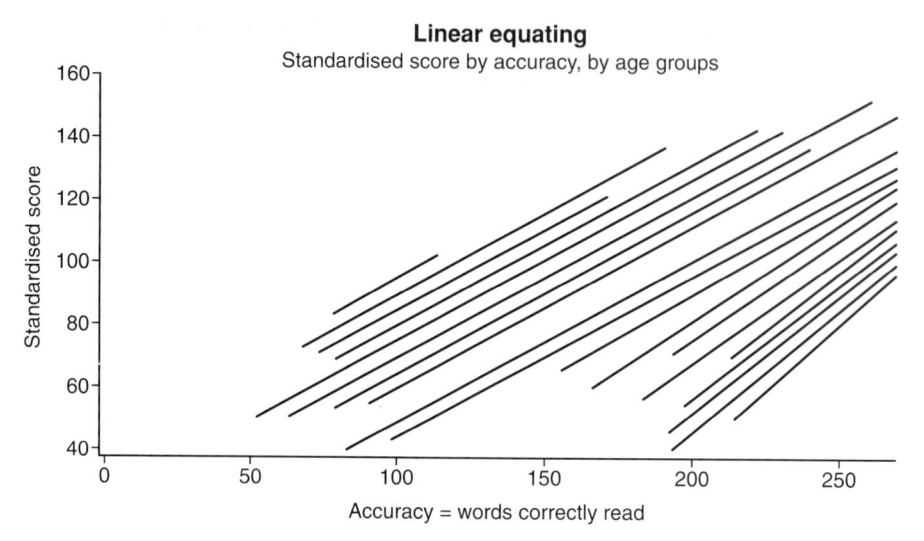

Figure 6.1: Linear equating performance by chronological age (the graph lines correspond to the age groups shown in Table 6.1)

chronological ages increased. It may be seen that there is a steady incremental progress, with a fallback between the primary and secondary age groups. This fallback, or dip, has been observed in a number of studies (Gray et al, 2003; Galton, Gray and Rudduck, 1999) and is associated with the transfer of pupils from primary schools to secondary school.

The words correctly read for each **percentile** shown in Table B are derived directly from the standardised scores in Table A. The 50th percentile (P50) in Table B corresponds to the Table A standardised score of 100, which is the central score at each age group in Table A. The P5, P10, P15, P20, P25, P30, P35, P40, P45, P50, P55, P60, P65, P70, P75, P80, P85, P90 and P95 percentiles correspond to the standardised scores 75.3, 80.7, 84.4, 87.4, 89.9, 92.1, 94.2, 96.2, 98.1, 100.0, 101.9, 103.8, 105.8, 107.9, 110.1, 112.6, 115.5, 119.2 and 124.7 which are based on the area under the standard normal (z) curve.

Pupils' **reading ages** were obtained by equating pupils' words correctly read on their *DRA* reading tests to the reading ages that they obtained on their *HGRT/ERT* equating tests.

Reliability

Reliability is concerned with the degree to which test scores are free from measurement errors, and can be determined by the relationships between scores from one occasion to another (*test-retest reliability*), from one form to another (*alternate-forms reliability*), or within one form (*internal consistency*). Reliability of the *DRA* has been found to be high using all three measures.

Test-retest reliability

Immediately prior to pupils' taking both their *DRA* Form A and Form B tests, they were asked to do one of five age-appropriate listening comprehension exercises A, B, C, D and E. Table 6.3 shows the mean and

Table 6.3: Means and standard deviations of listening comprehension scores

Listening comprehension exercise	before Form A			before Form B		
	n	Mean	SD	n	Mean	SD
A *(4 questions)*	45	3.5	0.7	22	3.3	0.6
B *(4 questions)*	147	3.4	0.9	160	3.5	0.8
C *(5 questions)*	118	4.1	1.1	113	4.4	0.7
D *(6 questions)*	75	4.6	1.1	78	4.9	1.0
E *(8 questions)*	46	6.4	2.0	58	6.8	1.6
All	*431*	*4.1*	*1.4*	*431*	*4.4*	*1.4*

standard deviation (SD) of the scores of 431 pupils who did both listening comprehension exercises.

The slight increase in mean scores for the listening comprehension exercises done before Form B is attributed to a combined 'learning and teaching effect' occurring between pupils taking their Form A and B tests.

Correlations can range from –1 (perfect negative correlation) through 0 (no correlation) to +1 (perfect positive correlation). Correlation values above +0.3 are considered to be reasonable, while correlations above +0.5 are considered to be very strong. Reliability values can range from 0 (no reliability) to +1 (perfect reliability); values above 0.7 indicate good reliability.

The Pearson's *r* correlation between pupils' two listening comprehension scores, or *test-retest reliability*, is 0.64. This suggests that teachers in the main did not have any difficulty in gauging pupils' ability and selecting the appropriate listening comprehension tests for them.

The Cronbach's Alpha reliability coefficient (taking pupils' first and second listening comprehension scores together as a combined two-item test) is also very good, at 0.78. Furthermore, using a 'strictly parallel model' there is an 'unbiased estimate of reliability' of 0.77. These measures, taken with the data in Table 6.3, support the view that the listening comprehension exercises provide a high and consistent level of discrimination between pupils of different abilities.

These data also support the view that pupils have approached both the *DRA* Form A and B tests with similar motivation. The correlation between pupils' scores on their first listening comprehension test and their *DRA* Form A test is 0.51, while the correlation between pupils' scores on their second listening comprehension test and their *DRA* Form B test is 0.44. These correlations suggest that pupils' scores on the listening comprehension tests are a reasonable predictor of their performance on their *DRA* test, and that teachers have, in the main, directed pupils to the appropriate Form A and Form B reading passages.

The Spearman-Brown formula (reported below) indicates that test reliability is related to test length; it is therefore reassuring to know that if the listening comprehension exercises had carried more available marks then all of the correlation and reliability measures mentioned here would have been significantly enhanced.

Alternate-forms reliability

It is possible to compare the comprehension scores of the same pupils from the first and second phases of the standardisation. These data provide alternate-forms reliability measures of the equivalence of Form A and Form B: three different measures of reliability are shown in Table 6.4.

Table 6.4: Alternate-forms reliability coefficients and standard errors of means

	Reliability coefficient	Spearman-Brown coefficient	Standard error of means Form A	Form B
Raw scores *(words correctly read)*	0.93	0.97	3.3	3.5
Reading comprehension scores	0.68	0.81	0.18	0.22
Listening comprehension scores	0.64	0.78	0.069	0.070

The *reliability coefficient* is the Pearson's *r* correlation of pupils' scores on Form A with their scores on Form B. The correlation values (on a scale of –1 to +1) here are all well above 0.5, which is considered to be a very strong correlation.

The *Spearman–Brown coefficient* is a reliability measure derived from a comparison of the variability of pupils' scores by considering Form A and Form B as two 'split halves' of the same test. The Spearman-Brown reliability values (on a scale of 0 to 1) here are all significantly greater than 0.7, which is considered to be very good.

The *standard error of means* measures how far the means of pupils' total scores for the Form A and B standardisation samples is likely to vary from the true population mean. The values shown here are all excellent, being very small indeed relative to the possible marks available in each test.

Internal consistency

Internal consistency reliability (Cronbach's Alpha) measures the homogeneity of items from a single test administration by relating the variance of individual item scores (i.e. the score for words correct on each of the three *DRA* assessed reading passages) to the variance of pupils' total marks. Hence it measures the reliability of the test as a whole. Internal consistency reliability coefficients were calculated separately for Forms A and B and for each age group. These coefficients are shown in Table 6.5.

Table 6.5: Internal consistency (Cronbach's Alpha) for Forms A and B, by age group

Age group	Form A	Form B
6:6–7:5	0.87	0.89
7:6–7:11	0.87	0.87
8:0–8:5	0.87	0.88
8:6–8:11	0.88	0.88
9:0–9:5	0.87	0.88
9:6–9:11	0.87	0.88
10:0–10:5	0.88	0.88
10:6–10:11	0.88	0.88
11:0–11:5	0.88	0.88
11:6–11:11	0.88	0.88
12:0–12:5	0.87	0.88
12:6–12:11	0.88	0.88
13:0–13:5	0.88	0.88
13:6–13:11	0.88	0.88
14:0–14:5	0.87	0.87
14:6–14:11	0.88	0.86
15:0–15:5	0.88	0.87
15:6–15:11	0.89	0.89
16:0–16:5	0.89	0.86
Overall	*0.88*	*0.88*

As can be seen, all of the Cronbach's Alpha values are very good (on a scale of 0 to 1, where 0.7 is usually considered to be quite acceptable). This is true not only for both Forms A and B overall (suggesting that both forms as a whole are internally very consistent and reliable), but also when broken down by age group, indicating that the various combinations of the *DRA* reading passages are also very reliable instruments for individual pupil assessment.

Validity

Criterion-related validity concentrates on whether test scores portray accurately an individual's ability on relevant criteria. One way that this can be examined is by correlating test scores with other tests that measure a similar ability or abilities that are assumed to relate closely to the one being measured. In the standardisation only a few of the administrators were able to provide recent scores from other published reading tests. Because the data is scant and at best could only be considered as indicative, it has not been reported. Many administrators were however able to provide the most recent National Curriculum level for each pupil: Table 3.5 (page 23) shows the link between reading ages and NC levels.

The *DRA* is unique in that it has been designed and written to match the National Literacy Strategy, whereas other reading tests are not designed in this manner and the teaching of reading may not be consistent with the way these tests have been designed to work. The *DRA*, for example, does not require the pupil to plod through the reading from the beginning until reaching material that is too difficult for them, or jumping in higher and having a notional basal score for the passages that are omitted. This combination of differences makes the issue of validity based on comparisons with other types of individual reading tests unlikely to be of critical significance.

Of more value to considering validity is the comparison of the performance of pupils on each raft of sub-sets of the test. The performance of these groups of pupils as shown by the graphs in Figure 6.1 indicate very similar performances no matter whether the test was for low levels of demand or medium or high levels of demand. The evidence indicates that the test design, which ensured that pupils met some easy reading, some more challenging text and some that they struggled with, has provided a valid set of measures.

References

Adams, M. (1990) *Beginning to read – thinking and learning about print*. Cambridge, Ma: MIT Press.

British Psychological Society. (1999) *Dyslexia, Literacy and Psychological Assessment*. Leicester: British Psychological Society.

Coltheart, M., Rastle, K., Perry, C., Ziegler, J. & Langdon, R. (2001) DRC. A dual route cascaded model of word recognition and reading aloud. *Psychological Review, 108*, 204–56.

Crumpler, M. & McCarty, C. (2004) *Nonword Reading Test*. London: Hodder & Stoughton.

Evans, B. (2001) *Dyslexia and Vision*. London: Whurr.

Galton, M., Gray, J. & Rudduck, J. (1999) *The Impact of Transition and Transfer on Pupil Progress and Attainment*, Research Report RR131, Nottingham: DfEE Publications.

Gray, J., Hussey, S., Charles, M. & Schagen, I. (2003) *Transfer and transitions in the middle years of schooling (7-14): continuities and discontinuities in learning* DfES Research Report 443, Chapter 2, pp.5-42.

Goswami, U. (1994) Reading by analogy: theoretical and practical perspectives. In C. Hulme and M. Snowling (eds) *Reading Development and Dyslexia*. London: Whurr.

Nation, K. (1999). Reading skills in hyperlexia: A developmental perspective. *Psychological Bulletin, 125 (3)*, 338–55.

National Literacy Strategy (1999 and 2000) *Progression in Phonics: materials for whole-class teaching*. London: Department for Education and Employment.

Nicolson, R. & Fawcett, A. (1990) Automaticity: a new framework for dyslexia research? *Cognition, 35*, 2, 159–82.

Oakhill, J. & Yuill, N. (2002) Research on young children: Learning to understand written language. In Wearmouth, J., Soler, J. and Reid, G. (eds). *Addressing Difficulties in Literacy Development: Responses at Family, School, Pupil and Teacher Levels*. RoutledgeFalmer (also in Funnell and Stuart).

Samuels, S., Shanahan, T. & Shaywitz, S. (2000) *Report of National Reading Panel. Teaching Children to Read: An Evidence-based Assessment of the Scientific Research Literature on Reading and its Implications for Reading Instruction. Report of Subgroup on Fluency*. Washington, DC: US Government Printing Office.

Snowling, M. (2002) Dyslexia: Individual and developmental differences. In R. Stainthorp & P. Tomlinson (eds). *Learning and Teaching Reading*. Leicester: British Psychological Society.

Stanovich, K. (1980) Toward an interactive-compensatory model of individual differences in the acquisition of literacy. *Reading Research Quarterly, 16*, 32-71.

Stanovich, K. (1991) The theoretical and practical consequences of discrepancy definitions of dyslexia. In M. Snowling & M. Thomson (eds) *Dyslexia: Integrating Theory and Practice*. London: Whurr.

Stanovich, K. (1998) Refining the phonological core deficit model. *Child Psychology and Psychiatry Review, 3*(1), pp 17-21.

Stothard, S. E. (1996) Assessing Reading Comprehension. In Snowling, M. & Stackhouse, J. *Dyslexia, Speech & Language*. London: Whurr.

Stuart, M. (2003) *Fine tuning the National Literacy Strategy to ensure continuing progress in improving standards of reading in the UK: Some suggestions for change.* (Retrieved 14th May 2004 from www.standards.dfee.gov.uk/pdf/ literacy/mstuart_phonics.)

Topping, K. (1995) *Paired Reading, Writing & Spelling*. London: Cassell.

Torgesen, J.K. (2002) Lessons learnt from intervention research in reading: A way to go before we rest. In R. Stainthorp and P. Tomlinson, *Learning and Teaching Reading*. Leicester: British Psychological Society.

University of Edinburgh (2002) *Edinburgh Reading Test 4*, third edition. London: Hodder & Stoughton.

Vincent, D. & Crumpler, M. (2000) *Hodder Group Reading Tests 1–3*. London: Hodder & Stoughton.

Wilkins, A., Lewis, E., Smith, F., Rowland, E. & Tweedie, E. (2001) Coloured Overlays and their Benefit for Reading. *Journal of Research in Reading, 21*(1), 41–64.

Wolf, M. & O'Brien, B. (2001) On issues of time, fluency, and intervention. In Fawcett, A. (ed) *Dyslexia: Theory and Good Practice*. London: Whurr.

Conversion Tables

Table A: Standardised scores for Forms A and B

The standardised score Table A is presented in shaded bands to aid interpretation. The central band includes all standardised scores that are within one standard deviation of the mean: standardised scores between 85 and 115 in this band reflect average performance in comparison with the standardisation sample. The intermediate band includes all standardised scores that are between one and two standard deviations of the mean: standardised scores between 70 and 84 in this band indicate well-below-average performance in comparison with the standardisation sample, whereas standardised scores between 116 and 130 indicate well-above-average performance in comparison with the standardisation sample. The outer bands include all standardised scores that are more than two standard deviations from the mean: standardised scores below 70 indicate very weak performance, whereas standardised scores above 130 indicate excellent performance.

Ensure that the raw score and chronological age of the pupil have been correctly calculated. Locate the raw score in the first column, then locate the column for the pupil's chronological age. Reading across the row, locate the standardised score in the column that corresponds to the pupil's raw score and record that score on the front of the *Pupil Record*.

Table B: Percentile scores for Forms A and B

Percentile scores indicate a pupil's position relative to all the other pupils in the same age group. For example, a pupil in the age group 10:0–10:5 who scores, say, 152 words correctly read is at the 30th percentile for that group, i.e. 30% of the pupils in that age group have scores that are worse (i.e. had fewer words correctly read) than our pupil.

Percentiles are sometimes reported as simply P25, P50 and P75 (called quartiles), but percentile steps of 5% are given here to provide a higher degree of discrimination between pupils of different reading abilities.

Table A: Standardised scores for Forms A and B

Words	6:6–7:5	7:6–7:11	8:0–8:5	8:6–8:11	9:0–9:5	9:6–9:11	10:0–10:5	10:6–10:11	11:0–11:5	11:6–11:11	12:0–12:5	12:6–12:11	13:0–13:5	13:6–13:11	14:0–14:5	14:6–14:11	15:0–15:5	15:6–15:11	16:0–16:5
300																128	125	123	
299																130	127	124	122
298																130	126	123	121
297																129	126	123	120
296																128	125	122	120
295															130	127	124	121	119
294															130	127	123	120	118
293															129	126	123	119	117
292															128	125	122	119	116
291														130	127	124	121	118	115
290														129	127	124	120	117	115
289														129	126	123	120	116	114
288														128	125	122	119	116	113
287														127	125	121	118	115	112
286														126	124	121	117	114	111
285														126	123	120	117	113	110
284													130	125	122	119	116	112	109
283													130	124	122	118	115	112	109
282													129	124	121	118	114	111	108
281													128	123	120	117	114	110	107
280													128	122	119	116	113	109	106
279													127	122	119	115	112	108	105
278												130	126	121	118	115	111	108	104
277												130	126	120	117	114	111	107	103
276												129	125	120	116	113	110	106	103
275												129	125	119	116	113	109	105	102
274												128	124	118	115	112	108	104	101
273				Standardised score above 130							130	127	123	118	114	111	107	104	100
272											130	127	123	117	114	110	107	103	99
271											129	126	122	116	113	110	106	102	98
270											129	125	121	116	112	109	105	101	98
269											128	125	121	115	111	108	104	101	97
268											127	124	120	114	111	107	104	100	96
267											127	124	119	114	110	107	103	99	95
266										130	126	123	119	113	109	106	102	98	94
265										130	126	122	118	112	108	105	101	97	93
264										129	125	122	117	112	108	104	101	97	92
263										129	125	121	117	111	107	104	100	96	92
262										128	124	120	116	110	106	103	99	95	91
261										128	124	120	115	109	106	102	98	94	90
260										127	123	119	115	109	105	101	98	93	89
259										127	122	119	114	108	104	101	97	93	88
258										126	122	118	113	107	103	100	96	92	87
257										126	121	117	113	107	103	99	95	91	86
256									130	125	121	117	112	106	102	98	95	90	86
255									130	125	120	116	111	105	101	98	94	89	85
254									129	124	120	115	111	105	100	97	93	89	84
253									129	124	119	115	110	104	100	96	92	88	83
252									128	123	119	114	109	103	99	95	92	87	82
251									128	123	118	114	109	103	98	95	91	86	81
250									127	122	118	113	108	102	98	94	90	86	81
249									126	121	117	112	107	101	97	93	89	85	80
Words	6:6–7:5	7:6–7:11	8:0–8:5	8:6–8:11	9:0–9:5	9:6–9:11	10:0–10:5	10:6–10:11	11:0–11:5	11:6–11:11	12:0–12:5	12:6–12:11	13:0–13:5	13:6–13:11	14:0–14:5	14:6–14:11	15:0–15:5	15:6–15:11	16:0–16:5

Table A: cont'd

Words	6:6–7:5	7:6–7:11	8:0–8:5	8:6–8:11	9:0–9:5	9:6–9:11	10:0–10:5	10:6–10:11	11:0–11:5	11:6–11:11	12:0–12:5	12:6–12:11	13:0–13:5	13:6–13:11	14:0–14:5	14:6–14:11	15:0–15:5	15:6–15:11	16:0–16:5
248									126	121	116	112	107	101	96	93	88	84	79
247									125	120	116	111	106	100	95	92	88	83	78
246									125	120	115	111	105	99	95	91	87	82	77
245									124	119	115	110	105	99	94	90	86	82	76
244									124	119	114	109	104	98	93	90	85	81	75
243									123	118	114	109	103	97	92	89	85	80	75
242									123	118	113	108	103	97	92	88	84	79	74
241									122	117	113	107	102	96	91	87	83	78	73
240									122	117	112	107	101	95	90	87	82	78	72
239									121	116	111	106	101	95	89	86	82	77	71
238									121	116	111	106	100	94	89	85	81	76	70
237									120	115	110	105	99	93	88	84	80	75	69
236									120	115	110	104	99	92	87	84	79	74	69
235								130	119	114	109	104	98	92	87	83	79	74	68
234								130	119	114	109	103	97	91	86	82	78	73	67
233								129	118	113	108	102	97	90	85	81	77	72	66
232								129	118	113	108	102	96	90	84	81	76	71	65
231								128	117	112	107	101	95	89	84	80	76	70	
230								128	117	112	107	101	95	88	83	79	75	70	
229								127	116	111	106	100	94	88	82	78	74	69	
228								127	116	111	105	99	93	87	81	78	73	68	
227								126	115	110	105	99	93	86	81	77	73	67	
226								126	115	110	104	98	92	86	80	76	72	67	
225							130	125	114	109	104	98	92	85	79	76	71	66	
224							129	124	113	108	103	97	91	84	79	75	70	65	
223							129	124	113	108	103	96	90	84	78	74	69		
222		Standardised score above 130					128	123	112	107	102	96	90	83	77	73	69		
221							128	123	112	107	102	95	89	82	76	73	68		
220							127	122	111	106	101	94	88	82	76	72	67		
219							127	122	111	106	100	94	88	81	75	71	66		
218							126	121	110	105	100	93	87	80	74	70	66		
217							126	121	110	105	99	93	86	80	73	70	65		
216						130	125	120	109	104	99	92	86	79	73	69			
215						130	125	120	109	104	98	91	85	78	72	68			
214						129	124	119	108	103	98	91	84	78	71	67			
213						129	124	119	108	103	97	90	84	77	70	67			
212						128	123	118	107	102	97	89	83	76	70	66			
211						128	123	118	107	102	96	89	82	75	69	65			
210						127	122	117	106	101	96	88	82	75	68				
209						127	122	117	106	101	95	88	81	74	68				
208						126	121	116	105	100	94	87	80	73	67				
207						126	121	116	105	100	94	86	80	73	66				
206					130	125	120	115	104	99	93	86	79	72	65				
205					130	125	120	115	104	99	93	85	78	71	65				
204					129	124	119	114	103	98	92	84	78	71					
203					129	124	119	114	103	98	92	84	77	70					
202					128	123	118	113	102	97	91	83	76	69					
201					128	123	118	113	102	97	91	83	76	69					
200					127	122	117	112	101	96	90	82	75	68					
199					126	121	116	111	100	95	89	81	74	67					
198					126	121	116	111	100	95	89	81	74	67					
197				130	125	120	115	110	99	94	88	80	73	66					
196				130	125	120	115	110	99	94	88	80	72	65					
195				129	124	119	114	109	98	93	87	79	72	65					
Words	6:6–7:5	7:6–7:11	8:0–8:5	8:6–8:11	9:0–9:5	9:6–9:11	10:0–10:5	10:6–10:11	11:0–11:5	11:6–11:11	12:0–12:5	12:6–12:11	13:0–13:5	13:6–13:11	14:0–14:5	14:6–14:11	15:0–15:5	15:6–15:11	16:0–16:5

Table A: cont'd

Words	6:6–7:5	7:6–7:11	8:0–8:5	8:6–8:11	9:0–9:5	9:6–9:11	10:0–10:5	10:6–10:11	11:0–11:5	11:6–11:11	12:0–12:5	12:6–12:11	13:0–13:5	13:6–13:11	14:0–14:5	14:6–14:11	15:0–15:5	15:6–15:11	16:0–16:5
194				129	124	119	114	109	98	93	87	78	71						
193				128	123	118	113	108	97	92	86	78	70						
192				128	123	118	113	108	97	92	86	77	70						
191				127	122	117	112	107	96	91	85	76	69						
190				127	122	117	112	107	96	91	85	76	68						
189				126	121	116	111	106	95	90	84	75	68						
188				126	121	116	111	106	95	90	83	75	67						
187			130	125	120	115	110	105	94	89	83	74	66						
186			130	125	120	115	110	105	94	89	82	73	66						
185			129	124	119	114	109	104	93	88	82	73	65						
184			129	124	119	114	109	104	93	88	81	72							
183			128	123	118	113	108	103	92	87	81	71							
182			128	123	118	113	108	103	92	87	80	71							
181			127	122	117	112	107	102	91	86	80	70							
180			127	122	117	112	107	102	91	86	79	70							
179			126	121	116	111	106	101	90	85	78	69							
178			126	121	116	111	106	101	90	85	78	68							
177		130	125	120	115	110	105	100	89	84	77	68							
176		130	125	120	115	110	105	100	89	84	77	67							
175		129	124	119	114	109	104	99	88	83	76	67							
174		128	123	118	113	108	103	98	87	82	76	66							
173		128	123	118	113	108	103	98	87	82	75	65							
172		127	122	117	112	107	102	97	86	81	75	65							
171		127	122	117	112	107	102	97	86	81	74								
170		126	121	116	111	106	101	96	85	80	74								
169		126	121	116	111	106	101	96	85	80	73								
168	130	125	120	115	110	105	100	95	84	79	72		Standardised score below 65						
167	130	125	120	115	110	105	100	95	84	79	72								
166	129	124	119	114	109	104	99	94	83	78	71								
165	129	124	119	114	109	104	99	94	83	78	71								
164	128	123	118	113	108	103	98	93	82	77	70								
163	128	123	118	113	108	103	98	93	82	77	70								
162	127	122	117	112	107	102	97	92	81	76	69								
161	127	122	117	112	107	102	97	92	81	76	69								
160	126	121	116	111	106	101	96	91	80	75	68								
159	126	121	116	111	106	101	96	91	80	75	67								
158	125	120	115	110	105	100	95	90	79	74	67								
157	125	120	115	110	105	100	95	90	79	74	66								
156	124	119	114	109	104	99	94	89	78	73	66								
155	124	119	114	109	104	99	94	89	78	73	65								
154	123	118	113	108	103	98	93	88	77	72	65								
153	123	118	113	108	103	98	93	88	77	72									
152	122	117	112	107	102	97	92	87	76	71									
151	122	117	112	107	102	97	92	87	76	71									
150	121	116	111	106	101	96	91	86	75	70									
149	120	115	110	105	100	95	90	85	74	69									
148	120	115	110	105	100	95	90	85	74	69									
147	119	114	109	104	99	94	89	84	73	68									
146	119	114	109	104	99	94	89	84	73	68									
145	118	113	108	103	98	93	88	83	72	67									
144	118	113	108	103	98	93	88	83	72	67									
143	117	112	107	102	97	92	87	82	71	66									
142	117	112	107	102	97	92	87	82	71	66									
141	116	111	106	101	96	91	86	81	70	65									
Words	6:6–7:5	7:6–7:11	8:0–8:5	8:6–8:11	9:0–9:5	9:6–9:11	10:0–10:5	10:6–10:11	11:0–11:5	11:6–11:11	12:0–12:5	12:6–12:11	13:0–13:5	13:6–13:11	14:0–14:5	14:6–14:11	15:0–15:5	15:6–15:11	16:0–16:5

Table A: cont'd

Words	6:6–7:5	7:6–7:11	8:0–8:5	8:6–8:11	9:0–9:5	9:6–9:11	10:0–10:5	10:6–10:11	11:0–11:5	11:6–11:11	12:0–12:5	12:6–12:11	13:0–13:5	13:6–13:11	14:0–14:5	14:6–14:11	15:0–15:5	15:6–15:11	16:0–16:5
140	116	111	106	101	96	91	86	81	70	65									
139	115	110	105	100	95	90	85	80	69										
138	115	110	105	100	95	90	85	80	69										
137	114	109	104	99	94	89	84	79	68										
136	114	109	104	99	94	89	84	79	68										
135	113	108	103	98	93	88	83	78	67										
134	113	108	103	98	93	88	83	78	67										
133	112	107	102	97	92	87	82	77	66										
132	112	107	102	97	92	87	82	77	66										
131	111	106	101	96	91	86	81	76	65										
130	111	106	101	96	91	86	81	76	65										
129	110	105	100	95	90	85	80	75											
128	110	105	100	95	90	85	80	75											
127	109	104	99	94	89	84	79	74											
126	109	104	99	94	89	84	79	74											
125	108	103	98	93	88	83	78	73											
124	107	102	97	92	87	82	77	72											
123	107	102	97	92	87	82	77	72											
122	106	101	96	91	86	81	76	71											
121	106	101	96	91	86	81	76	71											
120	105	100	95	90	85	80	75	70											
119	105	100	95	90	85	80	75	70											
118	104	99	94	89	84	79	74	69											
117	104	99	94	89	84	79	74	69											
116	103	98	93	88	83	78	73	68											
115	103	98	93	88	83	78	73	68											
114	102	97	92	87	82	77	72	67				Standardised score below 65							
113	102	97	92	87	82	77	72	67											
112	101	96	91	86	81	76	71	66											
111	101	96	91	86	81	76	71	66											
110	100	95	90	85	80	75	70	65											
109	100	95	90	85	80	75	70	65											
108	99	94	89	84	79	74	69												
107	99	94	89	84	79	74	69												
106	98	93	88	83	78	73	68												
105	98	93	88	83	78	73	68												
104	97	92	87	82	77	72	67												
103	97	92	87	82	77	72	67												
102	96	91	86	81	76	71	66												
101	96	91	86	81	76	71	66												
100	95	90	85	80	75	70	65												
99	94	89	84	79	74	69													
98	94	89	84	79	74	69													
97	93	88	83	78	73	68													
96	93	88	83	78	73	68													
95	92	87	82	77	72	67													
94	92	87	82	77	72	67													
93	91	86	81	76	71	66													
92	91	86	81	76	71	66													
91	90	85	80	75	70	65													
90	90	85	80	75	70	65													
89	89	84	79	74	69														
88	89	84	79	74	69														
87	88	83	78	73	68														
Words	6:6–7:5	7:6–7:11	8:0–8:5	8:6–8:11	9:0–9:5	9:6–9:11	10:0–10:5	10:6–10:11	11:0–11:5	11:6–11:11	12:0–12:5	12:6–12:11	13:0–13:5	13:6–13:11	14:0–14:5	14:6–14:11	15:0–15:5	15:6–15:11	16:0–16:5

Table A: cont'd

Words	6:6–7:5	7:6–7:11	8:0–8:5	8:6–8:11	9:0–9:5	9:6–9:11	10:0–10:5	10:6–10:11	11:0–11:5	11:6–11:11	12:0–12:5	12:6–12:11	13:0–13:5	13:6–13:11	14:0–14:5	14:6–14:11	15:0–15:5	15:6–15:11	16:0–16:5
86	88	83	78	73	68														
85	87	82	77	72	67														
84	87	82	77	72	67														
83	86	81	76	71	66														
82	86	81	76	71	66														
81	85	80	75	70	65														
80	85	80	75	70	65														
79	84	79	74	69															
78	84	79	74	69															
77	83	78	73	68															
76	83	78	73	68															
75	82	77	72	67															
74	81	76	71	66															
73	81	76	71	66															
72	80	75	70	65															
71	80	75	70	65															
70	79	74	69																
69	79	74	69																
68	78	73	68																
67	78	73	68																
66	77	72	67																
65	77	72	67																
64	76	71	66																
63	76	71	66																
62	75	70	65							Standardised score below 65									
61	75	70	65																
60	74	69																	
59	74	69																	
58	73	68																	
57	73	68																	
56	72	67																	
55	72	67																	
54	71	66																	
53	71	66																	
52	70	65																	
51	70	65																	
50	69																		
49	68																		
48	68																		
47	67																		
46	67																		
45	66																		
44	66																		
43	65																		
42	65																		
41																			
40																			
Words	6:6–7:5	7:6–7:11	8:0–8:5	8:6–8:11	9:0–9:5	9:6–9:11	10:0–10:5	10:6–10:11	11:0–11:5	11:6–11:11	12:0–12:5	12:6–12:11	13:0–13:5	13:6–13:11	14:0–14:5	14:6–14:11	15:0–15:5	15:6–15:11	16:0–16:5

Table B: Percentile scores for Forms A and B

Percentile	6:6–7:5	7:6–7:11	8:0–8:5	8:6–8:11	9:0–9:5	9:6–9:11	10:0–10:5	10:6–10:11	11:0–11:5	11:6–11:11	12:0–12:5	12:6–12:11	13:0–13:5	13:6–13:11	14:0–14:5	14:6–14:11	15:0–15:5	15:6–15:11	16:0–16:5
5th	<63	<73	<82	<92	<102	<111	<121	<130	<152	<161	<174	<190	<201	<212	<221	<226	<232	<238	<245
10th	63–73	73–82	82–92	92–101	102–111	111–121	121–130	130–140	152–161	161–171	174–183	190–198	201–209	212–219	221–227	226–232	232–238	238–244	245–250
15th	74–80	83–89	93–99	102–108	112–118	122–128	131–137	141–147	162–168	172–178	184–190	199–204	210–214	220–224	228–232	233–237	239–243	245–249	251–255
20th	81–85	90–95	100–105	109–114	119–124	129–133	138–143	148–153	169–174	179–183	191–195	205–209	215–219	225–229	233–236	238–241	244–247	250–252	256–258
25th	86–90	96–100	106–109	115–119	125–129	134–138	144–148	154–158	175–179	184–188	196–200	210–213	220–223	230–232	237–240	242–244	248–250	253–256	259–261
30th	91–94	101–104	110–114	120–123	130–133	139–143	149–152	159–162	180–183	189–193	201–204	214–216	224–226	233–235	241–243	245–247	251–253	257–258	262–264
35th	95–98	105–108	115–118	124–127	134–137	144–147	153–156	163–166	184–187	194–197	205–208	217–220	227–229	236–239	144–245	248–250	254–256	259–261	265–266
40th	99–102	109–112	119–122	128–131	138–141	148–150	157–160	167–170	188–191	198–200	209–211	221–223	230–232	240–241	246–248	251–253	257–258	262–264	267–268
45th	103–106	113–116	123–125	132–135	142–144	151–154	161–164	171–173	192–194	201–204	212–215	224–226	233–235	242–244	249–251	254–256	259–261	265–266	269–271
50th	107–110	117–119	126–129	136–138	145–148	155–158	165–167	174–177	195–198	205–208	216–218	227–229	236–238	245–247	252–253	257–258	262–263	267–268	272–273
55th	111–113	120–123	130–133	139–142	149–152	159–161	168–171	178–181	199–202	209–211	219–222	230–232	239–241	248–250	254–256	259–261	264–266	269–271	274–275
60th	114–117	124–127	134–136	143–146	153–155	162–165	172–175	182–184	203–205	212–215	223–225	233–235	242–244	251–253	257–259	262–263	267–268	272–273	276–277
65th	118–121	128–130	137–140	147–150	156–159	166–169	176–178	185–188	206–209	216–219	226–229	236–238	245–247	254–256	260–261	264–266	269–271	274–276	278–280
70th	122–125	131–134	141–144	151–154	160–163	170–173	179–183	189–192	210–213	220–223	230–233	239–242	248–250	257–259	262–264	267–269	272–274	277–278	281–282
75th	126–129	135–139	145–148	155–158	164–168	174–177	184–187	193–196	214–218	224–227	234–237	243–245	251–253	260–262	265–267	270–272	275–276	279–281	283–285
80th	130–134	140–143	149–153	159–163	169–172	178–182	188–192	197–201	219–222	228–232	239–241	246–249	254–257	263–266	268–271	273–275	277–280	282–284	286–28
85th	135–139	144–149	154–159	164–168	173–178	183–188	193–197	202–207	223–228	233–238	242–246	250–254	258–261	267–270	272–275	276–279	281–284	285–288	289–291
90th	140–147	150–156	160–166	169–175	179–185	189–195	198–204	208–214	229–235	239–245	247–253	255–260	262–267	271–275	276–280	280–284	285–288	289–293	292–296
95th	>147	>156	>166	>175	>185	>195	>204	>214	>235	>245	>253	>260	>267	>275	>280	>284	>288	>293	>296

Number of words correctly read

Appendix

Rules for selecting the second Reading (non-fiction) passage

Reading passage (age)	Length of passage (Words)	Numbers of errors in first fiction passage 10% or more — Go DOWN one level	Less than 10% — Go UP one level
2 (6–7)	25	3+	0–2
3 (7–8)	40	4+	0–3
4 (8–9)	40	4+	0–3
5 (9–10)	50	5+	0–4
6 (10–11)	50	5+	0–4
7 (11–12)	60	6+	0–5
8 (12–13)	60	6+	0–5
9 (13–14)	80	8+	0–7
10 (14–15)	100	10+	0–9
11 (15–16)	100	10+	0–9

Rules for selecting the third Reading (fiction) passage

Reading passage (age)	Length of passage (Words)	Numbers of errors in second (non-fiction) passage 10% or more — Go DOWN another level, or STAY on same level if came up previously	Less than 10% — Go UP another level, or STAY on same level if moved down previously
2 (6–7)	25	3+	0–2
3 (7–8)	40	4+	0–3
4 (8–9)	40	4+	0–3
5 (9–10)	50	5+	0–4
6 (10–11)	50	5+	0–4
7 (11–12)	60	6+	0–5
8 (12–13)	60	6+	0–5
9 (13–14)	80	8+	0–7
10 (14–15)	100	10+	0–9
11 (15–16)	100	10+	0–9

DIAGNOSTIC CHECKLIST

Pupil's name: **Date of Assessment:**

▶ **General background** *(make brief notes if appropriate)*

Sight and/or hearing difficulties:

Home language, if not English:

❑ *Tick if less than 2 years in English-speaking school*

Any interruptions during testing (e.g. a fire drill or noisy disturbance):

▶ **Pupil's response to the test** *(tick to indicate your rating of the pupil's performance on each aspect)*

confident	❑	❑	❑	❑	❑	❑	apprehensive
independent	❑	❑	❑	❑	❑	❑	requested help
commented on texts/illustrations	❑	❑	❑	❑	❑	❑	no engagement with texts/illustrations
focussed	❑	❑	❑	❑	❑	❑	distracted

Listening
listened attentively	❑	❑	❑	❑	❑	❑	lacked concentration

Reading
read with expression	❑	❑	❑	❑	❑	❑	read in a monotone
used clear voice	❑	❑	❑	❑	❑	❑	muttered
too slow	❑	❑	❑	❑	❑	❑	too fast
read in sentences	❑	❑	❑	❑	❑	❑	read word-by-word
self-corrected for meaning	❑	❑	❑	❑	❑	❑	lack of attention to meaning of text

Comprehension
referred back to text	❑	❑	❑	❑	❑	❑	answered from memory
gave extended answers	❑	❑	❑	❑	❑	❑	gave brief answers

Diagnostic Reading Analysis published by Hodder Education
Photocopies of this sheet may be made, for use solely in the purchasing institution.

▶ **Use of cues** *(tick as appropriate – see Manual, Chapter 4)*

	Uses effectively	**Uses ineffectively**	**Does not use**
Phonic cues	❏	❏	❏
Context cues	❏	❏	❏
Grammatical cues	❏	❏	❏
Graphic cues	❏	❏	❏

▶ **Patterns in performance** *(tick if one of these descriptors applies – see Manual, Chapter 5)*

❏   A pupil's reading accuracy and reading comprehension scores are both low *(page 41)*.

Reading Accuracy	Reading Comprehension
Very weak/Well below average	Very weak/Well below average

❏   A pupil's reading accuracy score is low, but his/her reading comprehension score is higher *(page 42)*.

Reading Accuracy	Reading Comprehension
Very weak/Well below average	Well below average/Average
(comprehension is better than accuracy)	

❏   A pupil's reading comprehension score is low, but his/her reading accuracy score is higher *(page 43)*.

Reading Accuracy	Reading Comprehension
Well below average/Average	Very weak/Well below average
(accuracy is better than comprehension)	

❏   A pupil's fluency/reading rate is low, but his/her accuracy and/or comprehension scores are higher *(page 44)*.

Reading Accuracy	Reading Comprehension	Fluency/Reading Rate
Well below average/Average **(better than fluency)**	Well below average/Average **(better than fluency)**	Very weak/ Well below average

▶ **Patterns in oral reading** *(tick if one of these descriptors applies – see Manual, Chapter 5)*

❏   Struggles with reading both simple regular words and common irregular words.

❏   Struggles with decoding many regular words, but reads common irregular words more quickly and accurately.

❏   Decodes uncommon regular words successfully, but unsuccessfully attempts to use phonics also to read common irregular words. Reading slow and laborious.

❏   Sounds out letters aloud successfully, but often cannot combine to form real words.

❏   Many errors make sense in context, but only one or two letters correspond to the actual word.

❏   Errors often result in non-words. Where they result in real words, they are unrelated to the context.

❏   Omits or confuses simple common words that *are* in his/her reading vocabulary, but successfully reads more complex words.

❏   Gives up quickly on words that he/she does not recognise at once. Does not attempt longer words at all. A high proportion of refusal errors to substitution errors.

Diagnostic Reading Analysis published by Hodder Education
Photocopies of this sheet may be made, for use solely in the purchasing institution.